White House
Usher

Stories from the Inside

Christopher B. Emery

Foreword by Barbara Bush

**

ISBN: 978-1-63492-656-0

Christopher B. Emery
Naples, Florida

Email: WhiteHouseUsher@gmail.com
www.WhiteHouseUsher.com

Ordering Information:
Quantity sales. Special discounts are available on quantity purchases by corporations, associations, and others. For details, contact the publisher at the address above.

Orders by U.S. trade bookstores and wholesalers. Please visit: www.WhiteHouseUsher.com

Printed on acid-free paper.

Publisher's Cataloging-in-Publication data
Emery, Christopher B.
White House Usher: Stories from the Inside / Christopher B. Emery
p. cm.
1. The main category of the book—History HF0000.A0 A00 2010
299.000 00–dc22 2010999999

Second Edition - October 2020

Dedicated to:

Katie Brooke
Waverly Grace
Parker Thomas

And

Isabelle

Acknowledgments

There are many I would like to thank for their encouragement, support, reviews, suggestions, debates, comments, and more. Most of all, when at one point I had decided to put my project on permanent hold, my partner Isabelle offered me the inspiration I needed to complete this. To you, Isabelle, I will always be grateful.

A man I look up to, Gary J. Walters, is the last of the truly great, qualified individuals to be a White House Chief Usher. Gary consistently performed at the highest level, superbly serving four presidents. Thankfully, he once saw something in a 28-year-old IT guy—me—and changed my life forever by providing a rare opportunity to work inside the White House, the home of America's First Family.

Thanks to my "sanity checkers"—family members, friends, and close colleagues who reviewed excerpts and provided feedback: Ariane Emery, Isabelle Hauswald, Edwin Huizinga, Keith Zumbrun, Al Salas, Scott Paton, Ian Komorowski, Denzil Thies, Andria Leo, Tam Stephanadis, and Brent Brookhart. Thank you all!

I acknowledge Angela Hoy of Booklocker.com who always quickly responded to my hundreds of emails and thousands of questions. And my editor Barbara McNichol was beyond wonderful in all aspects of helping me with this effort.

Thank you to Jean Becker, chief of staff to President George H. W. Bush. From her days in the White House until today, Jean has always been wonderfully helpful and supportive to me.

And finally, I dedicate this book to the individuals who inspire me beyond anyone else: my daughter Katie Brooke and my grandchildren Waverly Grace and Parker Thomas. This book is for you and future generations who will follow.

Cover Photo, Left to Right: Presidents Bush and Carter, author Chris Emery, Presidents Clinton, and Ford. Photo taken in the Red Room at the White House on Sept 13, 1993, day before the four Presidents signed the North America Free Trade Agreement. (Official White House photograph)

Back cover photo credit: Chaz Deausen

v

CONTENTS

Foreword

By Barbara Bush

Just the other day someone asked me what it was like to live in the White House with so much staff around all the time. Did you ever have a minute to yourself? Did you feel smothered by attention? Was there no sense of privacy?

My answer was immediate and heartfelt: We loved the wonderful White House staff. They were like family who somehow knew when we needed them but then magically disappeared when they knew we wanted to be alone. (Come to think of it, my children and grandchildren are not always so good at the "appearing" and "disappearing" business.)

The point being, they made life just about perfect every single day. Even when the problems of the country and the world weighed heavily on George's mind and shoulders, he knew he could come upstairs at the White House and feel at home.

At the center of the household activity is the White House Ushers Office, which oversees the 90-plus White House residential staff, including the plumbers and electricians, the chefs and the florists, the butlers and the housekeepers, and so many more. It is the ushers' job to keep everyone and everything running well and running on time. That would include the president and first lady.

With his book *White House Usher: Stories from the Inside*, former usher Chris Emery gives his readers a peek inside what happens upstairs at the White House. Chris's anecdotes tell a rich story of how America's house really is the first families' home. I loved my trip down memory lane.

He even tells a few stories on himself—including the night I caught him racing around upstairs in FDR's wheelchair.

Like so many of the White House staff, Chris became like family and deserves credit for being my very first computer guru. Even after we left town, I would call Chris and ask him to solve my computer issues. (And there were many.)

Enjoy your peek inside.

Barbara Bush

Preface

I've had a unique career, I spent 42 years in Information Technology, including 29 years with the federal government where I served as a Chief Information Officer at two agencies, a Chief Enterprise Architect at two agencies, and the head of software applications development. My start in the government is a rather unique story.

Here's what I mean. From 1986 until 1994, I served in the White House where three consecutive American presidents knew me on a first-name basis, and I've met seven of them: Nixon, Ford, Carter, Reagan, Bush, Clinton, and Bush. Daily, I encountered cabinet members, world leaders, movie stars, and professional athletes. No, I'm not a celebrity nor a big-time contributor, and I'm not a member of the media. Rather, I'm just average man who was in the right place at the right time.

Specifically, I served as a White House Usher. I had daily interaction with the president and first lady to ensure their needs were met for White House activities and events. As a White House Usher, I worked closely with the first family on everything from personal items to bringing up-to-date technology into the executive mansion; from managing events and ceremonies to the historic preservation of the executive mansion and its surrounding 18 acres. Primarily, I made sure the White House safeguarded the privacy of members of the first family while making them feel at home.

Starting in January 1986, I was busy automating the White House Travel Office (which later became infamous). In 1987, I coordinated the press setup in the White House for the Reagan/Gorbachev Summit. In 1993, President Clinton invited me to partake in a group photo with four presidents (I used the photo for my book cover). A year after that, I helped Mrs. Barbara Bush use her laptop computer and, well, more about that later.

After my eight years in the White House, I worked at the opposite end of Pennsylvania Avenue. I routinely walked through the historic corridors of the U.S. Capitol building, passing members of

Congress and their staffs. I remember seeing Senator Ted Kennedy, his head down looking serious. Early one morning on the Senate subway, seated directly across from me was Senate Majority Leader Bill Frist. We practically touched knee-to-knee as we each stared intently into our Blackberry devices until we finally looked up and smiled at each other. Late one evening, again riding the Senate subway, there was only one other rider and they occupied the car directly in front of me—Senator Hillary Clinton.

I'd never would know whom I might run into each day as I headed to my office. The 100 Senators I found easy to identify, many seeming like movie stars, while House members appeared more like regular people and were harder to recognize. With 435 members of the House, who can possibly keep track of them all?

Years later in 2014, from the historic corridors of the Robert F. Kennedy Department of Justice building, President Obama's Attorney General Eric Holder congratulated me at a Great Hall ceremony with an award for Excellence in Leadership. Amazingly, I've had a career of extremes. In 1994, I became the only White House usher in the 20th century to be terminated (a story you'll read about). But later, I had the honor of the Department of Justice recognizing me for excellence in leadership.

Only in America!

Chris Emery
October 2020

Introduction

The Ushers Office provides oversight and management for the White House Executive Residence, its staff, and surrounding 18 acres of grounds. The ushers have more access to the president than most members of the family and are responsible for taking care of the first family's most secluded area—their home. Because their privacy is paramount, little is known about the ushers who work there.

However, it's truly one of the best jobs in existence. I was extremely grateful to have been able to work in this position. I was honored to have met seven presidents and work directly for three of them—Ronald Reagan, George H. W. Bush, and Bill Clinton. Hired in 1986, I was only the 18th usher since 1891 and became the only one to be fired during the 20th century in March 1994 (more on that later). Immediately after my termination, I was inundated with calls from members of the media wanting inside information about the White House and the first family. I also received calls from literary agents asking me about writing a book. Really? My priority was getting back to work to take care of my own family.

Since then, however, I pondered what I'd actually write if the time came. Yes, it would be about the history of the Ushers Office and anecdotes from my experiences there, without revealing anything too personal about any of the first families. During my eight years in the White House, I had taken detailed notes and began to review them, putting together ideas. Immediately after my firing, members of the media kept pressing me for information. Imagine, a camera crew even showed up on my front porch! (I declined their interview request.) A reporter from the United Kingdom came, too, and offered money. I turned her down and showed her the door. The great author Tom Clancy reached out to me and offered advice on writing a book; he also encouraged me to call his agent, which I did.

Over time, I got several appointments with a senior officer of a large New York publishing firm. I also met with numerous publishers and literary agents. Everyone wanted the "inside scoop" and, specifically, any dirt I could dish out. They also wanted me to strike while the iron was hot, make headlines—anything that would sell books. One firm quoted me a six-figure advance and put together samples of stories *I* would write.

Well, once these agents and publishers understood I wouldn't write anything that might infringe on the first family's privacy in a negative way, they abruptly lost interest. They told me they had a bottom-line focus, and if I couldn't provide a quick-turnaround, revealing, hot-selling book, then they wouldn't pursue anything else with me. Tom Clancy's agent told me my writing samples were "too Reader's Digest." How many millions of people read *Reader's Digest*? Still, subsequent calls and letters to *Reader's Digest* editors went unanswered.

Although the literary experts didn't want my story, whenever any Washington gossip about the White House surfaced, I'd get calls from leading members in the media. I was interviewed once each on ABC's Nightline, Good Morning America, and Dateline NBC plus three times by the FBI and twice by Congressional committees.

Ultimately, I decided to do this project as a collection of personal stories and self-publish under my terms—no agents, no New York publishers, no advances, and NO TRASH. The stories you'll read don't focus on a specific president or political ideology or philosophy. I have absolutely no political aspirations, nor do I have any vendettas. What I have is a unique and interesting insight into one of the most fascinating places in existence—The White House, 1600 Pennsylvania Avenue, Washington, DC.

The Ushers Office

In September 1985, I felt content at my job as a computer software manager in Greenbelt, Maryland. I had no plans to move on; however, at lunch one day I was flipping through the *Washington Post* and found the following ad in the classified section:

THE WHITE HOUSE
EXECUTIVE OFFICE OF THE PRESIDENT
OFFICE OF ADMINISTRATION is seeking a
Computer Specialist to perform office automation . . .

Wow! Wouldn't it be great to get a rejection letter from the White House, something on White House letterhead! I'd have fun showing it off to my office colleagues, imagining I'd say, "Hey guys! Look who wrote to me!"

I quickly printed out my résumé on a dot matrix printer—that old green-bar tractor-fed computer paper—and threw together a cover letter and mailed it off. Then I waited and waited. Nothing. Eventually, I'd forgotten all about it until one evening in December 1985, the phone rang. My family and I were seated at the dinner table, and my 12-year-old stepdaughter answered. Her eyes got as big as saucers as she handed the phone to me, whispering, "It's the White House." Figuring it was a joke, I tried to think of an appropriate impersonation-voice to answer with—Arnold Schwarzenegger, Jimmy Carter, Ronald Reagan, or Henry Kissinger? (I could do all of them fairly well.) But I decided to be myself and play along with the "prank."

"Hello, this is Chris Emery," I said, then listened intently as the caller identified herself as someone from the White House. Was I still interested in the position that I had applied for? When she referred to specifics from my résumé, I realized this was no joke!

So, I interviewed and landed the position starting in January 1986 as a Computer Specialist, GS-13 with a salary of $36,000. I became a member of the Reagan Executive Office of the President,

Office of Administration, working for the Information Technology Automated Systems Division. My office was in the New Executive Office Building—hardly the White House but considered part of the White House Complex. There, I was responsible for computer applications development for a variety of offices in the Executive Office of the President, including the White House Security Office, Executive Clerk's Office, White House Personnel, and the Travel Office. (It later became infamous during the Clinton White House due to a major ethics controversy. The scandal became known as Travelgate.)

My White House technology projects led to many early successes. For example, I installed the first computer network in an office of the president as part of a project that automated the Congressional bill tracking process. Another project automated the Executive Residence food and beverage inventory system, which meant setting up a system in the storeroom of the White House basement. Many people don't know that the first family pays for the food and supplies they consume. At that time, I developed a new application that replaced a nearly 200-year-old manual process. My system tracked the inventory used and produced a monthly bill that would be presented to the first family. I worked closely with the storeroom staff, the White House chefs, butlers, and Chief Usher Gary Walters.

This project was completed ahead of schedule and under budget. Toward its completion, I learned that one of the assistant ushers who'd been hired during the Kennedy administration was retiring, creating a rare vacancy in the Ushers Office. When the White House storeroom guys encouraged me to apply for the position, I thought, "What!? I'm on the leading edge of technology. I have a great future ahead in that field. Why on earth would I consider such an obscure job?"

Well, the more I learned, the more intrigued I became, and I asked Gary Walters if I could be considered. It truly was an opportunity of a lifetime—to serve in a role with such honor, tradition, and above all, trust.

What Exactly is the Ushers Office?

For more than 200 years, a small office has operated on the State Floor of the White House Executive Residence. Known as the Ushers Office, in 1994, it was still functioning much the same as it had for the previous 100-plus years to accommodate the personal needs of the first family and make the White House feel like a home.

The Ushers Office is the managing office of the Executive Residence and its staff of 90-plus. The staff consists of butlers, carpenters, grounds personnel, electricians, painters, plumbers, florists, maids, housemen, cooks, chefs, storekeepers, curators, calligraphers, doormen, and administrative support. Ushers work closely with the first family, senior staff, Social Office, Press Office, Secret Service, and military leaders to carry out White House functions: luncheons, dinners, teas, receptions, meetings, conferences, and more. Maintaining the entire 132-room mansion, preserving the fine arts collection, caring for the 18 acres of surrounding grounds, plus setting up for the 1.2 million annual tourists who come through the White House make up the diverse jobs on the Ushers Office's list of responsibilities.

Ushers Office circa 1989. Doorman Woodward Willoughby is standing; author Chris Emery is seated. (Note the Orioles game on the TV!) (Emery personal collection)

The ushers are always on hand for the arrival and departure of all first family members and guests. They field a variety of mail inquiries ranging from White House history and the fine arts collection to job opportunities. I started in the Executive Residence in March 1987, joining what I call the A-team: Chief Usher Gary Walters and three assistant ushers, James "Skip" Allen, Dennis Freemeyer, and me. At 29, I was the youngest member.

In his 40s, warm and charismatic, Gary Walters was a vibrant, passionate individual who took his role as chief usher seriously. Yet Gary had a wonderful sense of humor. A University of Maryland graduate, he had joined the Uniformed Division of the Secret Service in the 1970s and worked his way up to sergeant before being hired as an usher in the late 1970s. Becoming chief usher in 1986, he ran the White House well.

Skip Allen, age 40, had also come from the Secret Service. Skip's expertise was his in-depth and profound knowledge of the White House fine arts collection. Quite a character, he could appear eccentric and borderline pompous, yet in an endearing sort of way. He kept himself busy with an array of projects; he crocheted, sewed, and became the subject matter expert on the White House's rugs and draperies.

Dennis Freemeyer, age 34, had come to the Ushers Office from the National Park Service with an expertise in designing buildings. This studious, soft-spoken young man aspired to be an architect.

Our team worked well together, our hours were long, and every day we faced challenges and arduous tasks. We also knew how to play fun pranks on one another. Well, maybe I was more of a prankster than the others, but I quickly had them trained.

As the three assistant ushers, Skip, Dennis, and I worked on rotating schedules. It was a 21-day rotation that had each of us working evenings, weekends, and holidays. If a special event such as a state dinner was scheduled, all of us had to be on hand.

Administrative Usher Nancy Mitchell was also on our team. She held the Ushers Office together as a group. Pretty, with a wonderfully warm smile, Nancy had a southern charm that would melt anyone and prevented many from losing their tempers!

Supporting the Ushers Office was our de-facto assistant to the assistant usher, Worthington Wyatt White. As the White House Executive Residence budget administrator, Worthington would be on hand to help when we needed coverage in the office or for an event. Worthington, a former Virginia Tech football lineman was quite a character, carved quite an imposing figure at six-foot three, he was a big man.

This team became my family for the next seven years. We'd cover for each other and do whatever it took to take care of the first family's needs.

Each assistant usher had specific areas of responsibility. With my background in Information Technology (IT), I introduced computers and networks to the Executive Residence. Before I arrived, only one end-of-life IBM PC was being used in the White House Executive Residence. But when I left in 1994, I counted 35 PCs networked throughout the Executive Mansion from the lowest basement levels to the third-floor linen room.

In addition to my IT duties, I was the usher in charge of events, so I supervised a staff of 22—chefs, cooks, butlers, storeroom personnel, and florists.

***

A White House usher's job required long hours. Some days I arrived at 5:30 a.m. and didn't leave till 3 the next morning. But I didn't mind; the job was always exciting, and it thrilled me to witness history in the making.

Affectionately called the "A Team" are members of the Ushers Office from my years in the White House. L to R: Dennis Freemeyer, Skip Allen, author Chris Emery, and Gary Walters. Photo taken January 2012 at St. John's, Lafayette Square, Washington, DC. (Emery personal collection)

L to R: Dennis Freemeyer, Gary Walters, Nancy Mitchell, author Chris Emery, and Skip Allen, May 31, 1990 (Official White House photo)

White House Executive Residence

Friday, March 6, 1987 – *Transition from the Executive Office of the President to the Executive Residence*

It was my final day in the Reagan Executive Office of the President, Office of Administration. At 2 p.m. Sunday, I would report to my new job at the White House Executive Residence as the usher in charge of events. Chief Usher Gary Walters would have me shadow him and the others for as many as three months until I got up to speed. Determined to work hard, I wanted to be ready earlier than that!

In this complete career change, the thought of managing 22 people felt incredible. My new employees included the finest chefs in the world as well as butlers, florists, and storeroom personnel—all who had multiple years of White House experience. At age 29, I was younger than all of them.

In the weeks leading up to starting this new position, I read all I could find on the White House and its history. Now, I'd have the opportunity to witness history firsthand!

As I packed the final items from my office in the New Executive Office Building, I was feeling a nervous excitement. I might have landed on something so incredible, so challenging, so interesting that retirement in 30 years might seem too soon! It felt reassuring to know that if my White House Ushers Office position didn't work out, I still had my information technology experience to fall back on.

As I thought more about my short time in the Executive Office of the President, one of the more memorable events was the Tower Commission, created by President Reagan in response to the Iran Contra scandal. The commissioners operated in the New Executive Office Building on the floors directly above the office I was now leaving, and the commission members and I often rode in the elevator together. Released February 26, 1987, the Tower Commission's report blamed everyone involved and criticized the president's management style. As a result, White House Chief of Staff Donald Regan was replaced by former Senator Howard Baker.

Baker was stellar—a former Tennessee senator who, during the 1973 Watergate Hearings, became famous for having asked, "What did the president know and when did he know it?" I really liked this solid individual who was known for honesty and fairness. This move seemed to have approval from all sides. "Maybe now things will get back to normal," I thought. *Washington Post* had a photograph of President Reagan coming out of the Old Executive Office Building along with aides Tom Dawson and Jonathan Miller, my former boss's boss. Interestingly, an unrelated article next to Baker's photo stated Baker would set up a fresh team.

***

It had been thrilling to work in the Office of Administration for the previous 14 months, but the years to follow couldn't parallel anything I could possibly imagine. Being the only person who was technical yet understood the business customers, I'd be leaving quite a void.

At 2 p.m., I went to the White House Residence for an appointment to sign documents, get my parking permit, and basically prepare for my Sunday start. Unfortunately, my new boss, Chief Usher Gary Walters, wasn't present; he was upstairs in the private residence meeting with Mrs. Reagan. So, I was escorted to the East Room and watched what appeared to be utter chaos—all sorts of lighting and sound crews and guys setting up a stage while others were cleaning. They were preparing for Sunday's performance at the White House starring Bobby Short, Liza Minnelli, and Vic Damone for a tribute to Rodgers and Hart, American songwriters from the 1920s and 30s.

I walked next door to the Green Room where veteran usher Skip Allen and others were placing plastic sheeting on the walls to protect the wallpaper. The room had been completely emptied of its furnishings and artwork. Starting Monday the wood floor, installed during the Truman renovation, would be replaced.

I stood around trying to look official and wise, then walked back into the East Room and chatted with Art Nock, a salty veteran White House electrician. Back at the Ushers Office, I saw retiring Usher Nelson Pierce, the man I was replacing. He gave me my East Executive Avenue parking permit then showed me the route to take from where I'd park on East Executive Avenue. I'd go through the East Wing into the ground floor of the Executive Residence, then up to the state floor and the Ushers Office.

The visit to the Executive Residence left me with a feeling of trepidation and second-guessing. I questioned, "What the heck am I getting myself into?" Because of this complete career change, and with so few having any familiarity with the job of an usher, my closest friends and family could offer no practical advice. I wondered, "Am I making the right decision?"

Sunday, March 8, 1987 – *My First Day in the White House Executive Residence*

On that beautiful, sunny 70-degree day, I left my house in Maryland at noon. Katie, my two-year old daughter, stood at the top of the driveway wearing an adorable pink dress and waving a small American flag. How could she comprehend where her father was going?

I drove to my old office in the New Executive Office Building and collected a few remaining items, then drove to my new parking spot on East Executive Avenue. Because a car was in my space, I drove back to the new Executive Office Building, parked in the basement garage, and walked over to the White House. I had butterflies as I walked up the north drive, looking at the amazing view of the north facade of the White House. With each step I became more comfortable. "I can't believe how fortunate I am," I kept thinking.

I climbed the steps and onto the North Portico, took in a deep breath, and then walked in through the front door. From the grand foyer, I could see WETA Public Television's large crew setting up lighting, sound, and camera equipment. I walked into the Ushers

Office where several staff members greeted me before getting back to reviewing the plans for the late-afternoon performance.

***

At 3:07 p.m., Mrs. Reagan came down to the East Room and watched the final minutes of the rehearsal, then posed for photos with Composer Marvin Hamlisch. Twenty minutes later, she went back upstairs.

At 4:30, the 176 guests began to arrive in the East Room. A few minutes before 5 p.m., Gary Walters and I stood outside its pocket doors to await President and Mrs. Reagan. When Gary asked if I'd like to see the show, I said yes and, with reluctance, took a seat near the rear of the East Room. I was torn between seeing the show or staying with Gary to get a close-up view of President and Mrs. Reagan. I figured I'd have many chances to see the first family, so I sat in the last row and watched an excellent production! I wasn't too sure how this 1930s music would appeal to most people in the audience, but the Reagans sure loved it.

After the show, the guests and performers lined up to meet the President and First Lady. I wisely didn't get in the receiving line— certainly not appropriate for an employee!

Monday, March 9, 1987 – *Senate Hearing*
Bright and early Monday, I arrived at the White House before 7 a.m. and parked on East Executive Drive. The big event that day was going to Capitol Hill for the Senate budget hearings on the White House Executive Residence. I sat in the Dirksen Senate Office Building room SD-192 with Executive Residence Budget Administrator Worthington White and National Park Service executives Jack Fish and Jim McDaniel. Before the White House Executive Residence came up on the agenda, I heard fascinating presentations from the General Services Administration, National Archives, National Security Council, and my former agency, the White House Office of Administration.

The National Park Service executives representing the Executive Residence along with Worthington presented our budget to the committee chairman Senator Dennis DeConcini. Our budget was very different from the agencies that had just presented. Because we represented the president's home and were last to present (right after the National Security Council was grilled), we had it pretty easy. The senator asked questions about a few maintenance and restoration projects, but it seemed he asked out of curiosity rather than due diligence.

Worthington and I returned to the White House Executive Residence at 12:30 p.m. As soon as I got back, I met Maureen Reagan, the daughter of President Reagan and his first wife, actress Jane Wyman. Maureen greeted me warmly and rather boisterously. I could tell she was quite a character.

Tuesday, March 10, 1987 – *Meeting the First Lady*
Tuesday's highlight was meeting First Lady Nancy Reagan late in the afternoon. Gary Walters and I went upstairs to see her just as she was preparing to come down to the ground floor library for an interview taping. She seemed preoccupied but was pleasant and greeted me warmly. My hand retained the smell of her hand lotion for hours afterward.

The remainder of the week was intense with learning and meeting people, plus Gary gave me a fascinating tour of all eight levels of the White House. I did see First Lady Nancy Reagan a few more times and looked forward to meeting the president.

Monday, March 16, 1987 – *Meeting the President!*
Wow! What a way to start out the week. On this Monday, no doorman was on duty, so the president needed an escort to go to the Oval Office. I asked Gary who should go up to get him. "We will!" he replied. At 8:52 a.m., I met the 40th President of the United States. Gary introduced us, President Reagan and I shook hands, and the president said with a smile, "Welcome aboard."

"Good handgrip," I thought. With broad shoulders and perfect posture, the president was bigger than I'd imagined. A handsome man, President Reagan had deep lines on his face. He did look old but healthy and strong. I imagined he had a lot on his mind, including a possible press conference midweek.

Tuesday, March 17, 1987 – *"Happy St. Patrick's Day, President Reagan!"*

Again, no doorman on duty, so I greeted the president on my own. Feeling nervous, I went upstairs at 8:49 a.m. and waited with the Secret Service Presidential Protective Detail agent and one of the president's valets. I kept going over how to operate the elevator so we wouldn't stop on any wrong floor. (The White House elevator has a special key that ushers use when transporting a member of the first family. Use of this key would by-pass those floors designated by the Secret Service for automatic opening.)

Stepping out of the elevator, I opened the double doors that led to the hallway to the private residence. A few moments later, I heard footsteps. President Reagan looked surprised to see me. When I said, "Good morning, sir," he replied, "Good morning" in a raspy voice. I then added, "Happy St. Patrick's Day!" He responded with a "thank you" as he entered the elevator. I fumbled with the controls, but I got us going. I remembered to hit the movement buzzer three times to signal the Secret Service that President Reagan was on his way. I turned and smiled to the president who was wearing a bright green tie. "Nice tie," I said. He laughed and said, "I get to wear it once a year." As he walked through the elevator doors and headed toward the West Wing, I said to him, "Have a nice day" then thought, "Okay, Chris, you're talking way too much" as President Reagan disappeared into a mass of aides and agents.

Wednesday, March 18, 1987 – *Preparing for a State Dinner*

I arrived late this day—at 11:50 in the morning—because I knew I'd be staying late to watch the rehearsal dinner we'd serve to President and Mrs. Reagan. This would prepare us for the March 31st State Dinner. Rehearsal dinners provided an opportunity for the chefs to prepare and receive feedback on the meal for the upcoming event.

After the dinner, Mrs. Reagan came into the second-floor kitchen wearing a robe and slippers, she conferred with Gary Walters,

Executive Chef Henry Haller, and Pastry Chef Roland Mesnier. She loved everything. This confirmed we were ready for the big event.

Thursday, March 19, 1987 – *My First Reagan Press Conference*
I arrived at 11:30 a.m. and put in my longest day thus far, working until 11 p.m. The press conference was at 8 p.m. and the White House Press Corps stampeded in at 7:30 like a herd of cattle. At 7:45, President Reagan came down to the Old Family Dining Room next to the Ushers Office to meet with senior staff. Every so often I could hear a roar of laughter. At 30 seconds past 8 p.m., the president walked through the Ushers Office, stumbled on a chair pad, then looked at me and said with a laugh, "I better not do that out there."

Watching from the TV in the Ushers Office, I thought the press conference went well. President Reagan communicated in a strong and deliberate way. After Helen Thomas, the dean of the press corps, announced its conclusion, she then suddenly lunged forward with a question. About a dozen reporters followed her, all yelling as the president backed down the hall. When he came back through the Ushers Office, Chief of Staff Baker exclaimed, "You did a lot better out there than in our rehearsals!" The president quipped, "That's because your questions were a lot tougher than theirs!"

The president then thanked his senior staff and headed to the elevator saying, "Now I'll go upstairs and see what I said" referring to the evening's news recaps. Everyone laughed.

My first six weeks had gone well—so well that I started regular shifts on my own a full six weeks ahead of schedule. I would no longer be doubling up with the usher on duty for training.

Richard M. Nixon

Richard M. Nixon circa 1987 (Official White House photo)

Tuesday, April 28, 1987 – *Nixon's Poignant Visit*

I greeted former President Nixon as he arrived at the White House shortly before 5 p.m.—his first solo trip since he resigned and left in disgrace on August 9, 1974.

President Nixon arrived in a single government car. As he got out, he looked at me, smiled, and said hello. He was wearing a dark suit similar to those he wore in every image I'd ever seen of the man. We entered the White House Diplomatic Reception Room where he was greeted by Chief of Staff Howard Baker and National Security Advisor Frank Carlucci. As we walked into the ground floor hallway, Nixon paused and sighed as he looked around, reacquainting himself with the once-familiar surroundings.

We took the elevator to the private quarters where President Nixon met with President Reagan for 70 minutes. When the meeting had concluded and as President Nixon came off the elevator on the ground floor, Chief of Staff Howard Baker asked if he could take a photo of the former president in front of the portrait of his wife, former First Lady Pat Nixon. President Nixon looked in admiration at the portrait, then remarked that he'd never seen it and said how much he liked it. Known for being a camera buff, Baker had his camera at the ready and snapped a few photos. We then walked out to the South Portico where a car waited. No fanfare, no press entourage, and no throngs of staffers lining the driveway. Only a single car and an old man leaving the south grounds in obscurity.

I thought back to the last time President Nixon left through these doors on that dismal day in 1974, all those frozen-in-time iconic images, his forced smile from the top step of Marine One, waving vigorously, then with arms spread, flashing his famous two-handed peace salute before disappearing in the chopper as a broken man.

Learning the Ropes

Monday, May 18, 1987 – *Panic Alarm!*

    While I sat at my desk in the Ushers Office at 8:50 a.m., a Secret Service agent from the Presidential Protection Detail ran up the steps saying an alarm went off in the first lady's study. Initially, I stared blankly at this stressed-out agent and then he dashed up the steps to the private quarters. What kind of alarm went off—smoke alarm, door alarm? What should I do? I then ran up the steps and found the agent, plus one other agent and our old doorman, Roland Harley, who was waiting for the president.

    I asked the agents where this "immediate response alarm" or "panic alarm" came from. They replied, "The first lady's study." I immediately walked through the West Sitting Hall and to the first lady's private office, figuring this must be what they refer to as the study. As I got there, a maid was walking out. "Good," I thought. "That's what it was. The maid must have bumped something and set off the alarm by accident."

    I wheeled around and went back to near the elevator where the agents still looked panicked. The door man, Mr. Harley then pointed to the dressing room door and said, "That's the study." I figured, "Heck, I'm the new guy here. Mr. Harley who's been around since Moses must know what he's talking about." So off I again, this time to the door he pointed to.

    I knocked lightly and Mrs. Reagan answered, "Yes?"

    "Mrs. Reagan?" She again answered, "Yes."

    For the life of me, I couldn't figure out where on earth her voice was coming from!

    "Mrs. Reagan, it's me, Chris."

    She again said, "Yes."

    "Where are you?"

    She said, "I'm in here."

    By this time, I was well into the hallway. To my right was her bathroom and the bedroom was to the left. There, I found Mrs.

Reagan lying in bed watching ABC's *Good Morning America* with their dog Rex beside her.

I stepped in and asked, "Is everything okay?" She looked surprised and said "Yes." That's when Rex began his regular attack on the intruder—ME!

I yelled over Rex's barking, "I'm sorry to bother you, but we got a distress signal and I just wanted to be sure everything was alright."

I walked in reverse out of the room, knowing not to turn my back on Rex or I'd risk getting bitten.

Shortly after, I kept thinking about how Mrs. Reagan might be upset by my intrusion. But she just lay there very relaxed in a white silk nightgown with cold cream around her eyes. I was the one who was upset.

I related the entire incident to Gary Walters, who assured me I acted properly. The first lady had requested the installation of the "panic alarm" system after the president's colon surgery. Then Gary described other false alarms in the Residence, including some in the middle of the night with no ushers on duty. The Secret Service agents had to go up alone and check things out.

***

At 11:30 a.m. that day, guests were arriving on the State Floor of the White House for the Senate Ladies Luncheon. At the same time there was a Rose Garden event; the E-star Awards ceremony to recognize U.S. businesses that had made significant contributions to the American export industry.

A call from the northwest gate told me a visiting general had been misdirected and was coming up to the North Portico. I figured the general must be part of the Rose Garden event and not the Senate Ladies Luncheon. I went out to the Grand Foyer of the State Floor where the general had just entered. The military aides on hand to help with the Senate Ladies Luncheon looked much relieved to see me since they weren't quite sure where to seat the general. I said to the general, "Why don't you come with me, sir?" And off we went, down the back stairs, out through the Palm Room and into the Rose Garden.

The president had just begun to address the audience. I led the general around the back of the two-tiered press platform and we stood behind the 150 seated guests.

As he eyed the press, the general looked upset. "Are the press supposed to be coming to the luncheon?" he asked. I assured him that not everyone will get into the luncheon. He had a very puzzled look on his face and asked, "The press corps are coming to the Carlucci lunch?"

"Carlucci lunch!?"

"Yes. That's why I'm here—to meet with the national security advisor in the Roosevelt Room."

Whoops! We had to make a rapid retreat. I thought, "How do I get this guy down the Colonnade and into the West Wing while the president is in the middle of his remarks?" Then I looked up to see press taking our photograph. We made a hastened dash up the Colonnade and into the West Wing without too many noticing.

***

Earlier this week, assistant usher, Dennis Freemeyer had gone upstairs to get President Reagan. The president got into the elevator and stood toward the back as an agent stepped on. Then the president said to no one in particular, "That damn Jim!" Dennis froze, thinking the president's aide, Appointments Secretary, Jim Kuhn, must have done something wrong. "That damn Jim!" the president repeated. As they reached the ground floor, the president quipped, "That darn gym! My chest is getting too big." President Reagan had been prescribed a strict regimen of physical exercise (mostly bench pressing) after an assassin made an attempt on his life in 1981. I'm told he'd increased his shirt size by three sizes!

Wednesday, October 21, 1987 – *Mrs. Reagan Hospitalized*
On this day, Mrs. Reagan had a mastectomy to remove her left breast due to breast cancer.

Dear Mrs. Reagan,
I was happy to learn of your progress from your husband.

It will be great to have you back home.
Sincerest Wishes,
Chris

I sealed the envelope and wrote "Mrs. Reagan" on it. President Reagan would be leaving soon and, on his way to the motorcade, he'd tell the press that the first lady would come back with him tomorrow morning. Ever since her mastectomy, the president traveled to Bethesda Naval Hospital each evening, departing about 5:30 and returning around 8:15.

Earlier when I went upstairs to get him, President Reagan got on the elevator, smiled, and said hello as Presidential Appointments Secretary Jim Kuhn reviewed the next day's schedule with him. Stepping closer to the president, I waited for my chance. When he looked up, I handed him my envelope and said, "Sir, could you please give this to the first lady?" He replied, "Sure" and put the envelope into his right suit jacket pocket. The elevator doors opened and out we went.

A few hours later when the president returned, I asked (as I had the previous two nights) about Mrs. Reagan. He responded, "Good, but anxious to be coming home." I wondered if he delivered my note. He didn't say.

The next night, I escorted Chief of Staff Senator Howard Baker, Deputy Chief of Staff Ken Duberstein, the president's physician Dr. Hutton, and Presidential Appointments Secretary Jim Kuhn to the second floor to get the president for his press conference. Standing outside the elevator, I could hear Senator Baker talking to the first lady. She went to her husband's bathroom door, knocked, and said, "Honey, everyone is here." As she turned back toward the hallway, she saw me, smiled, and said, "Thank you for your note." I replied, "Thank you for coming back." (I thought, "Oh man! That's the best I could come up with!?")

Mrs. Reagan graciously responded, "Well, I'm thankful to be back."

***

The previous Friday, President Reagan met with Soviet Foreign Minister Eduard Shevardnadze and announced that the Soviet leader Mikhail Gorbachev would visit the White House on December 7th for a Nuclear Arms Reductions Summit.

Late October 1987 – *Staff Evaluations*

I managed a staff of 22 that included five chefs, five butlers, four kitchen workers, five florists, and three storeroom personnel. These seasoned White House veterans had an average tenure of more than 15 years. Feeling fortunate to have a good group of people working for me, I wanted the employee evaluations to complement each individual's accomplishments and provide feedback for any possible areas for improvement.

The performance reviews had gone well, with only one left to conduct and that was for Sous Chef Hans Raffert. Hans was the heir apparent to the executive chef position occupied by Henry Haller, who had retired in June after 21 years of flawless service. The White House sous chef since 1969, Hans was an excellent chef, but on too many occasions, he could be a bit too demanding of his subordinates and anyone within earshot. So, what happened?

The two of us were seated practically nose to nose in the tiny desk area adjacent to the main kitchen. At age 30, I was relatively new to the Ushers Office while Hans, age 60, had started his career as a chef apprentice when he was 14. While I clearly pointed out that his work product was exemplary, I decided to offer counsel by suggesting he improve his communications skills and his tact, diplomacy, and temperament.

Hans became enraged. He declared that at no time during his 46 years of experience had he ever received anything but an outstanding review and had never received any suggestions for improvement. My explanation fell on deaf ears. Visibly upset, Hans shouted, "I HAVE NEVER BEEN ANYTHING BUT OUTSTANDING, AND IF YOU DON'T REMOVE YOUR STATEMENTS ABOUT MY NEEDING IMPROVEMENT, I WILL GO DIRECTLY TO MRS. REAGAN AND OFFER MY RESIGNATION. HOW WILL YOU HANDLE THAT!?"

On second thought, Hans ended up with an outstanding performance rating.

Wednesday, November 11, 1987 – *Veterans Day Snowstorm*
In a freak, record-setting snowstorm, 10 to 14 inches of snow had fallen. My drive to the White House for my afternoon shift was better than it might have been since I'd recently purchased a sturdy four-by-four vehicle and because it was Veteran's Day, a federal holiday, there was little traffic.

During the late afternoon, with the North Portico lights on, the view from the Ushers Office was beautiful—a winter wonderland. All was quiet, I was getting caught up on answering letters on behalf of President and Mrs. Reagan. Typically, these letters contain questions about the fine arts collection, historic events, or state dinner menus. My favorite letters came from elementary school students and were usually about pets or White House trivia. One young lady wrote that she wanted to be a chef when she grew up and she would like to meet the White House chef. I arranged for her and her parents to meet him. Their absolute excitement and appreciation made it all worthwhile.

At 10 p.m., I received a call from Mrs. Reagan who said, "Chris, there's a rubbing-like noise in our bedroom." I replied, "I'll be right up."

What the heck could it be? Did it again have to do with the contractors working on the tunnel project? As I walked into the second-floor hallway, I could hear the president's TV blaring in the study. I found Mrs. Reagan in the West Sitting Hall and, typical of any night before she traveled, she was rushing around. The following morning, she'd be off to Indianapolis for a 'Just Say No' drug program event.

She looked up to see me, smiled, then said, "Right in here." We walked into the bedroom. Right away I heard next to her desk a wall thermostat that was hissing. I turned to her and said, "That's strange. I'll have one of the engineers check it immediately."

Back in the Ushers Office, I called the White House engineer. Sam Henry, on the night-shift, answered. After I described the noise to him, he said they'd had problems with the old heating system the last few days due to warm weather. They'd put overrides in the system because one system came from the ceiling and the other from the window. I'm thinking, "How will I explain all this to Mrs. Reagan when she asks? She's not at all mechanically inclined, and I'm not much better when it comes to these antiquated systems!"

After Sam made a few adjustments, I went back upstairs to check it out. I knocked on the bedroom door, which was open. I could see the president in bed, knees propped up supporting a stack of papers on his lap. "Come in," Mrs. Reagan said. I walked across the room and pointed to the thermostat, which was completely silent, and said, "Well, that's better." Mrs. Reagan then asked, "What was the problem?" I stuttered as I attempted to explain what little I understood. Just as I had gotten my lines straight, Rex—their darling troll of a dog—awoke from his bed in the first lady's dressing room. As he came running in barking and snarling, the president attempted to swat him with a handful of papers, yelling "REX, SHUT UP!!" I said rather loudly, "It was the valve that needed adjustment." With that, I got a nod of acknowledgment from the first lady, who probably couldn't hear a word. Quickly, I backed out of the room so that little varmint Rex couldn't bite me from behind. Damn that dog!

The Soviets

December 7-10, 1987 – *The White House Soviet Summit*
The White House Soviet Summit would consist of a series of meetings hosted by President Reagan and attended by General Secretary Mikhail Gorbachev. It would allow the two leaders to discuss regional conflicts in Afghanistan, Central America, and Southern Africa as well as arms control for chemical and conventional weapons, the status of Strategic Arms Reduction Treaty (START) negotiations, and human rights. However, their top priority was working out the Intermediate-Range Nuclear Forces (INF) treaty.

What follows are my notes from the hours leading up to the Summit and the Summit itself.

Monday, December 7, 1987 10:51 p.m.
On the eve of the Summit, I was in the ushers' basement suite, having arrived at the White House shortly after 6 a.m. I was on my feet this entire 16-hour day. To this point, I was involved in practically every aspect of this historic event. I decided to spend the night at the White House so my travel wouldn't be delayed by all the extra security surrounding the White House.

The annual Christmas tree lighting ceremony had been held earlier that evening. From my perfect vantage point in the Green Room, I stood behind the president and first lady as they went out onto the terrace, then watched them on the White House Communications monitor. Through the Green Room window, I could see the unlit Christmas tree on the Ellipse outside of the White House grounds. President Reagan pushed the historic button that's been used since President Hoover to light the tree. Once he pushed it, an electrician in a trailer near the tree threw the real switch. Voila! The beautiful tree came alive with thousands of lights.

The Soviet Summit required weeks of planning and preparation involving the White House National Security Council (NSC), Press Office, senior aides, State Department, Secret Service, Military, and Social Office. At 9 p.m., we had our final planning meeting, this time including the Soviet "diplomats" (also known as the KGB).

In preparation for the next day's treaty signing, the actual treaty document was placed on an historic table in the East Room. This table had been first used by President Andrew Johnson for his cabinet and later by President William McKinley for signing the Peace Protocol between Spain and the United States on August 12th, 1898. (Media reports erroneously stated it was President Lincoln's cabinet table.)

As part of the planning, I sat at the table at Reagan's place while a Soviet participant stood in for Gorbachev. Suddenly, a heated discussion ensued about a minor interpretation of a phrase in the treaty. U.S. National Security Council and State Department representatives haggled with the Soviets over a couple of words and haggle they did. I worried that everything would unravel. Fortunately, after several minutes, a compromise was reached. We made promises that the official copy to be signed would include the changes everyone had agreed to.

Tuesday, December 8, 1987

I showered and got to the office at 6:25 a.m. Having slept in the ushers basement suite, the commute wasn't bad; I had to wait 12 seconds for the elevator and the ride from the sub-basement to the State Floor took another 15 seconds. It was a cool and clear morning. Chief Usher Gary Walters called saying his alarm hadn't gone off, but he was on his way. This is precisely one of the reasons I chose to sleep at the White House!

By 7 a.m., guests began arriving on the South Grounds well in advance of the arrival ceremony. With all the extra security throughout the city, many decided to get an early start. The Soviet motorcade arrived a few minutes after 10 a.m. I watched from the Green Room, and then I moved to the Blue Room to have a picture-perfect view. Various members of the Executive Residence staff stood there, too. Gary had asked assistant usher, Dennis Freemeyer and me to be available after the South Lawn ceremony to get the coats of the principals as they entered the Diplomatic Reception Room. I headed down and watched the remainder of the ceremony from the Diplomatic Reception Room just inside the double doors to the South Grounds.

Before long, both leaders had completed their speeches. As they headed toward the entrance, I stationed myself near the door to the South Portico ready to assist. Upon entering, I took President Reagan's coat, and one of his valets, appearing from nowhere, quickly took it from me. I stepped forward to help Mrs. Gorbachev with her coat when a KGB agent abruptly brushed me out of the way and helped her instead.

The special invited guests and senior VIPs then entered the hallway and were guided to the State Floor for a receiving line. After the receiving line, President Reagan and General Secretary Gorbachev went to the Library on the ground floor where veteran White House photographer Bill Fitzpatrick was set up to take their photo. Speculation abounded as to how the two leaders would get along. From my vantage point, as they left the Library for the Oval Office, Reagan was noticeably taller than Gorbachev. Gorbachev appeared pleasant (he smiled as he passed me) and Reagan looked confident and relaxed. I could tell already that the two of them were getting along well.

Meanwhile, the first lady and Mrs. Gorbachev were served tea and coffee in the Green Room. That prompted me to check out the South Portico, knowing the first lady would be bringing Mrs. Gorbachev down after their tea to see her off. I was shocked to see everything in disarray; no one had been made aware of the impending South Portico departure. I immediately corralled Secret Service and grounds crew to move the stanchions from the earlier ceremony, and clear the South Drive of the cables, podiums, and other things. I then helped get Mrs. Gorbachev's three-car motorcade into position. The General Secretary's motorcade was already forming for his later morning departure from the Oval Office, making my maneuvers a challenge, especially since the gigantic Soviet Zil limousines were the size of oil tankers!

It took forever (it seemed) to get Mrs. Gorbachev's small motorcade into position around the General Secretary's 18-car motorcade. I felt like I was directing traffic on a busy airport runway! Everything came together just in time as the first lady escorted Mrs. Gorbachev to the South Portico. General Secretary Gorbachev left a short time later. They would both be back at the White House at 1:30 p.m. for the INF Treaty signing.

My primary responsibility during the Summit was to coordinate and monitor the media. What a fiasco! At 1:10 p.m., the guests began to arrive for the 1:30 East Room treaty signing. At 1:28 the president and first lady stood in the Diplomatic Reception Room waiting for the Gorbachevs to return. Standing with them, we waited and waited. At 1:40, the first lady said, "That's it. I'm sitting down." She sat in the chair nearest me.

A few seconds later, someone announced, "Here they are." The president looked over to the first lady. He had both arms extended as he motioned with his hands and said, "Come on, honey." As the Gorbachevs entered, the general secretary paused in front of me. I reached for his coat. Before I could get my second hand on it, a KGB agent brushed me back.

The principals were led to the Red Room before being escorted to the East Room. I stood in the Grand Foyer. Once the first lady and Mrs. Gorbachev were seated in the East Room, assistant usher, Skip Allen and I opened the large East Room doors. This way, the TV audience had a view of the Cross Hall with its long red carpet. The Marine Band was poised, and Frank Urban from White House Communications announced, "Ladies and Gentlemen, the President of the United States and the General Secretary..." The band played "Ruffles and Flourishes," then the "Presidential March" as both men walked the long hallway to the dais in the East Room. They each made remarks, then sat at the historic Andrew Johnson Cabinet Table. It was the very table where I'd sat the night before when the treaty verbiage dispute was resolved.

President Reagan and General Secretary Gorbachev each signed the INF Treaty a total of 16 times, exchanged pens, shook hands, and applauded each other. Then they stood and exited, going straight to the opposite end of the hallway, the State Dining Room. I stood by in the Grand Foyer as they walked by. What a moment!

Signing the INF Treaty, East Room, December 8, 1987 (Official White House photo)

White House East Room immediately after the signing of the INF Treaty. President Reagan and General Secretary Gorbachev applaud each other, December 8, 1987 (Official White House photo)

With a roaring fire in State Dining Room fireplace, President Reagan spoke first. I left the room and watched the speeches from the Usher's Office TV while the audience in the East Room watched live on large monitors. At the conclusion of the address, the networks switched back to the East Room. The still-photographers then poured into the State Dining Room to snap photos.

I could see from the Ushers Office TV that Mrs. Reagan and Mrs. Gorbachev were sitting in the East Room, although they should have already exited. Before I could react, Gary had already taken off for the East Room where, seconds later, Mrs. Reagan and Mrs. Gorbachev were escorted out. The doorman took them down in the elevator to the Diplomatic Reception Room for Mrs. Gorbachevs second departure of the day. We then opened the State Dining Room doors for the photographers to exit. And exit they did, in a rush. Gary and I stood just outside the hallway next to the elevator as Gary pounded on the button to call the elevator to the State Floor. But evidently the doorman had locked the elevator on the ground floor!

Gary flew down the steps (did his feet even touch a step?). As it turned out, the doorman was a little slow at the controls. The elevator came up as Gary was flying down. The doors opened just as the president and general secretary approached. They entered the elevator, followed by an interpreter, an agent, then me. The two leaders were laughing and joking as we went down, they were clearly getting along well.

***

With the leaders headed for the Oval Office, I went back to the State Floor to oversee the process of clearing out the media, cameras, cables, and lighting so the state dinner setup could begin. The interpreters' booth was the last item to leave the State Dining Room. With close to 30 butlers and staff working together, it took us less than an hour to set up the dining room with 13 round tables, place-settings, flowers—the works!

The schedule of the evening had to be adjusted because the Soviets insisted on being out of the White House by 10 p.m. Typically, state dinners and post-dinner entertainment go until 11 p.m. or even longer. Everything was condensed to meet their demands for an earlier departure.

By 5:30 p.m., I was worn out. That's when I went to our basement suite to change into my tux for the dinner. I turned on the TV and watched as local news reported there would be two nervous individuals at the White House tonight: entertainer-pianist Van Cliburn and White House Chef Jon Hill, making his State Dinner debut. No doubt, Jon was an experienced Executive Chef but not a hands-on type of chef as, say, the recently retired great Henry Haller. Jon Hill's hiring as executive chef was a surprise; everyone had expected Sous Chef Hans Raffert to be promoted. Jon was good at directing the staff, but he lacked the critical ability to pitch in with the actual cooking. Thus, his tenure at the White House turned out to be short-lived.

As for Van Cliburn, what a fun person! He felt quite honored and, yes, quite nervous to perform for these world leaders. Van Cliburn could be called a perfectionist, which made the evening especially exasperating for us, the ushers.

***

The guests started arriving at 6:15 p.m. At 7:05 p.m., the president and first lady stood poised in the Diplomatic Reception Room waiting for the tardy Soviets. Ten minutes later, as the Gorbachevs entered, I got two hands on Mrs. Gorbachev's sable coat before I was again brushed away by the KGB. Darn, I thought I had a good position—like playing center in basketball. I just needed to do a better job of blocking out.

The pre-dinner receiving line took longer than expected as the principals happily chatted with the guests. Dinner was served close to 7:30 after both leaders gave lengthy toasts.

Suddenly we faced a time crunch! After encouraging guests to move swiftly to the East Room as soon as dinner ended, I took my post in the doorway to the East Room. As was customary, the principals were holding in the Red Room until all the guests were seated. President and Mrs. Reagan, General Secretary and Mrs.

Gorbachev were announced, walked in, and sat down. Then, Van Cliburn was announced.

"How could this guy who won the Tchaikovsky Award in 1958 look so young?!" I thought. His performance was spectacular. As it concluded, President Reagan went on stage to thank Van Cliburn, who then hugged the Gorbachevs and played a sing-along of "Moscow Nights" in Russian. What a scene.

At 10:46 p.m., the Reagans escorted the Gorbachevs via elevator to the Diplomatic Reception Room for their departure. This was 45 minutes later than the Soviets had demanded. But while the KGB seemed troubled by it, General Secretary and Mrs. Gorbachev were clearly enjoying themselves.

***

As the Soviet couple approached the door to the South Grounds, I realized I had taken Mrs. Reagan's shawl from her when the Gorbachevs had arrived earlier that evening. Having left it in Gary's office, I immediately turned on my heel, ran up the back stairs, grabbed the shawl, and dashed back down to the Diplomatic Reception Room in time to see the president and first lady walk out to the South Portico. On this cold night, I suspected Mrs. Reagan would freeze. As I opened the doors, I was immediately blinded by the press lights. Once I adjusted, I walked up to Mrs. Reagan and asked if she would like to have her shawl. She said yes with a shiver, so I draped it around her and left. Mission accomplished.

The evening ended in the Ushers Office with the ushers, an electrician, doorman, members of the social office, and Jack Courtemanche (Mrs. Reagan's chief of staff) toasting with Summit Cuvee—the wine used for the formal toast earlier. Then Gary gave each of us a bottle as a thank you.

Wednesday, December 9, 1987
This was the day for the First Ladies Tour. Mrs. Reagan met Mrs. Gorbachev and walked her through the Ground and State Floors; then they had coffee in the Red Room. However, this visit didn't go well for Mrs. Reagan. She stumbled badly recounting historic facts

and looked outmatched compared to Mrs. Gorbachev, who had done her homework.

Later that night, the president and first lady attended a reciprocal dinner at the Soviet Embassy. Once they returned to the White House at 10:15, I was free to head home.

Thursday, December 10, 1987

On this cloudy morning, I left home at 10:05 and used my White House credentials to get through all the heavy security. It started with Metropolitan Police roadblocks near the White House, then Park Police checkpoints, and finally the U.S. Secret Service—guys I knew well. I made it to my space #15 on East Exec at 10:55—not bad considering all the security checks.

That morning, General Secretary Gorbachev was due to arrive at 11. I checked in at the Ushers Office, did a quick walk-through, and headed to the South Grounds with Gary. By then, it was 11:35 and General Secretary Gorbachev still hadn't arrived. We got word that Vice President George Bush was at the Soviet Embassy in final negotiations on a matter with Gorbachev.

Finally, the Soviets' motorcade arrived at noon. Motorcade? More like a Red Army parade! I stood at the South Portico watching in amazement as 40 cars just kept rolling by, one after another.

***

Back in the Ushers Office, Dink the electrician was asking about contingency plans for moving the departure ceremony indoors if it started to rain. "No," I responded, "it won't rain that hard." Social Secretary Linda Faulkner dashed back and forth while the wonderful, elegant Assistant Social Secretary Cathy Fenton stayed cool and collected as usual. Linda and I went into the Old Family Dining Room to make a slew of seating adjustments for the working luncheon, which was hosted by President Reagan and attended by the General Secretary Gorbachev and senior staffs from both sides.

At 12:20 p.m., the two leaders and their entourages were seated. The luncheon broke about 1:55 and Mrs. Gorbachev arrived at the North Portico five minutes later. This time, I didn't even attempt to help her with her coat!

***

Back in the office, Gary walked in and told me to pull the curtains closed because Chief of Staff Senator Howard Baker was using the phone below the TV. I shut the curtains, thinking, "Why am I closing these for the Chief of Staff?" then I turned and saw President Reagan. He smiled, nodded, then looked tersely at his chief of staff. He said, "What the hell is the hold up? Get them over here; we've got thousands of people waiting." I didn't know who he was referring to. But right away, Senator Baker got off the phone and, walking with the president, headed to the Library for a meeting. Meanwhile, Gorbachev had gone to the Map Room. The two sides were trying to work out something.

***

I looked out the window and saw rain. At that point, close to a thousand people had gathered on the South Lawn. Whatever might had been in dispute with the two leaders was settled, and at 2:15 p.m., the president and general secretary met in the Diplomatic Reception Room. Three minutes later, they were joined by Mrs. Reagan and Mrs. Gorbachev.

All the ushers and some of the butlers had huddled in the Diplomatic Reception Room near the South Portico doors. Gary was reviewing our umbrella assignments as if he were coaching a sandlot football team. He whispered that he didn't think it would look good for African-American butlers to be holding umbrellas for these world leaders. I thought, "True, we'd look like the last plantation!" Gary, Dennis, and I would handle it. I'd cover Mrs. Gorbachev, Dennis would cover President Reagan, Gary would cover Mrs. Reagan, and Steve, a military aide, would cover General Secretary Gorbachev.

The doors opened and out we walked into the rain holding out our umbrellas. I joked that the KGB would tackle us before we got to the end of the red carpet.

The next thing I knew, we were walking toward the stage—all of us covering the closest dignitary. So much for our plan. As we got on stage, I saw the president standing at the podium *uncovered*. How did this happen!? I quickly reached out and covered him with my umbrella while the first lady stood to my left holding her own umbrella.

As I stood there, I tried not to think of the millions of TV viewers and the immense history of this moment. Instead, I fixed my eyes on the back of the president's collar. What an honor to see this important event from this perspective!

***

I stood on stage for almost 20 minutes, my arm ready to fall off from fatigue. I shifted hands while the translations took place. Then I noticed the water dripping off my umbrella onto the president's fountain-pen-written note cards. The letters were blurring together. Oh no! Still, I couldn't get any closer. The president noticed and calmly placed his note cards in his vest pocket as he continued his remarks, never missing a beat.

L to R: General Secretary Gorbachev, President Reagan, author Chris Emery, Mrs. Reagan, December 10, 1987 (Official White House photo)

When the president concluded his remarks, he stepped back. I did too as he joined Mrs. Reagan under her umbrella. Then at the back of the stage, Appointment Secretary Jim Kuhn frantically waved me down from the podium. As I stepped down, Steve, the military aide, motioned for me to cover Gorbachev, who was getting rained on. But because I was too far away, Dennis Freemeyer stepped up and covered him. After everyone had stepped down from the dais, I covered General Secretary and Mrs. Gorbachev as they approached their limo. The Reagans and the Gorbachevs stood together and said their goodbyes. Several times, they said, "See you in Moscow!" And off they went.

As I walked back into the White House, I hung onto my umbrella like a football player holding on to the ball after scoring the winning touchdown. Back in the Ushers Office, we celebrated with high-fives all around. What a day! What a WEEK!

Close Call

Tuesday, February 2, 1988 – *A Slight Snag*

I was sitting at my desk in the Ushers Office at about 6 p.m. The president and first lady were scheduled to go to a Republican National Committee (RNC) dinner shortly. The phone rang. Maureen Reagan. Could someone help with her dress? I said I'd help. She hesitated and said yes but then asked if any maids were available. I promised I'd have someone stop in. But I called everywhere; the maids must have been in Timbuktu, so I thought, "I'd better get up there. Maureen is one person you don't want to keep waiting."

I knocked on the Lincoln Bedroom door and Maureen replied, "Come in."

"Maureen, it's Chris." When she explained she needed her dress zipped up in the back, I thought, "No problem." Well, I started to zip and damn, it got snagged less than halfway up! "Oh, my gosh, now what?" All I could think was she'd miss the dinner because I ripped her darn dress.

I frantically worked on it and kept trying, knowing Maureen wasn't pleased nor patient. She warned me, "Be careful; it's chiffon!" Trying to conceal my fear, I thought I'd make conversation. "Maureen, are you going to the same dinner as President and Mrs. Reagan?" She looked over her shoulder as if I had two heads and said, "Of course. I'm hosting the dinner!" My thoughts kept spinning. "Way to go, Chris. She's the co-chair of the RNC so of course she'd be hosting the RNC dinner, you idiot!"

So much for idle conversation. The zipper appeared hopelessly snagged, run aground, off track, like the Titanic—a big-time catastrophe! Just when I was about to plead my case, I heard a knock at the door and turned to see one of the maids, Ivanez. "Thank you. There is a God!" I thought.

To Ivanez, I said, "Come on in!" I showed her my predicament without words. It took Ivanez all of five seconds to save my life. I wanted to kiss her! As quickly as I could, I back-pedaled out of the room and high-tailed it out of there. Whew!

Press Conference and Head of State Visits

Wednesday, February 24, 1988 – *White House Rules Not Always Followed*

Setting up for the evening's press conference, I had a run-in with a CBS lighting man. I never liked this guy; he was arrogant and challenging. He always argued against the rules we'd put in place to protect the White House furnishings and fine arts collection. That included no duct tape on the floor or touching the furniture, keeping the light towers far from the paintings, cleaning up after themselves, and more. This lighting man could be called the worst, especially compared with the absolute best in the business, Marvin Purbaugh of NBC-TV.

Marvin showed great pride in the White House and cared deeply for its historic items. It showed in his superior work. When Marvin handled the lighting, "hot spots" never showed up on the president. By comparison, the lighting crew from CBS lacked ability, and the head of the crew was just plain nasty. He told me he'd been doing lighting since I was in diapers. I thought in response, "No doubt you did an awful job of it back then, too!"

***

Overall, other than poor lighting, the press conference went well. When it ended, I headed toward the Red Room to meet the president and escort him upstairs. I looked back at the Ushers Office to see electrician Bill Cliber frantically motioning me to return. When I got there, he told me the operator had the first lady on the phone, calling from New York. She was holding for the president. So, I brought President Reagan into the Ushers Office where he picked up the phone. I closed the curtains in the window to prevent anyone from the outside seeing in. I gathered Mrs. Reagan must have told him he finally got it right (referring to his quick exit at the end of the press conference) because I heard him reply in protest, "That wasn't the only thing I did right!"

They spoke for a few minutes, then said their "I love you's" before ending the call—a cute exchange.

Friday, February 26, 1988 – *A Cancellation Means a Lot of Notifications*
The operator's line rang. I answered and she said, "The president is calling."

"Yes, sir, this is Chris."

President Reagan said, "Chris, could you please let the appropriate people know that we're not going to Camp David this weekend. I just finished talking to Nancy. With her coming back tomorrow and all that's going on, we've decided to stay here."

"Yes sir, I'll take care of it."

"Thank you."

"Yes, sir."

I then phoned the admin operators, Presidential Aide Jim Kuhn, Secret Service Presidential Protective Detail PostW16, Uniformed Division Command Center 058, White House Chef, Chief Usher Gary Walters, Operations, Engineers, White House Communications, Camp David, and the first lady's chief of staff. Mission accomplished!

Sunday, March 6, 1988 – *"Just let me look."*
At 6:08 p.m. at my desk in the Ushers Office, it was quiet except for the squawking of the Secret Service Uniformed Division radios. President and Mrs. Reagan were upstairs, not at Camp David. For the second weekend in a row, they had stayed at the White House. In the news:
- Bush wins South Carolina primary; Super Tuesday is two days away.
- U.S. steps up its pressure on Noriega.
- Israel's West Bank situation worsens.
- Iraq and Iran are firing missiles at one another's capital cities.
- Iran fired on U.S. helicopters.

In White House news, Sous Chef Hans Raffert was officially promoted to executive chef, replacing Jon Hill who had replaced the legendary Chef Henry Haller, who had joined the White House in 1966 and retired on October 1, 1987. Chef Raffert had a different demeanor than Chef Haller, and some found him difficult to be around, but he was an outstanding chef.

***

The night before, I went up to escort the president and first lady over to the East Wing theater to watch home movies. Dressed in a navy-blue robe and pajamas with a red sash, the president looked cool, like a Ninja warrior. The first lady wore dark slacks and a knee-length sweater. She also sported a dark mark on her upper lip after visiting the doctor's office earlier that day.

As we headed to the East Wing Colonnade, amazingly Mrs. Reagan acted like a tourist, taking advantage of the quiet to peer into the China Room, then across the hall and into the Library. Next, she slowed down to look at all the exhibits along the East Colonnade. The president seemed impatient, thinking she was holding things up. As he stood in the doorway to the theater, she was marveling at the drawing of the Harrison Blue Room. When the president said, "Well, let's go in," she replied, "Honey, I'm not hurting anything; just let me look." She came upon current photos and exclaimed, "There we are with Gorbi (Gorbachev)!"

Shortly after, they entered the theater and I closed the door. I thought, "I wish they would walk through the entire house and enjoy what's there." Every time they go anywhere, a half-dozen agents and staff surround them, which ruins any possibility for them to slow down and enjoy walking through the White House.

Monday, April 11, 1988 – *Tree or Ferns?*

On my first night back from vacation, President and Mrs. Reagan were hosting the King and Queen of Sweden. Fifteen minutes before the first guest arrival, Alfredo, one of the butlers, called me with a "panic" message. Mrs. Reagan wanted the small tree moved in the Yellow Oval Room, so their royal guests could stand on the

Truman Balcony. As I entered the Yellow Oval Room, I noticed on the right, an open door to the president's study. Walking up to the potted tree, I thought, "How the heck can I get rid of this heavy potted tree and where will I put it?" I suddenly looked up to see the President and Mrs. Reagan. I said, "I'll take care of the tree."

Mrs. Reagan looked puzzled, then pointed to the window and said, "What I said was get rid of these potted ferns." At this point, Gary Walters entered and we both carried away the four ferns as Mrs. Reagan said, "I want the guests to be able to see the tulips on the South Grounds."

With all four ferns removed, the first lady disappeared through the study doors as President Reagan, Gary, and I stood admiring the view to the south. The president said, "I'm reading Gore Vidal's *Lincoln*. Vidal couldn't have known Washington or the view from up here because Vidal describes Lincoln looking out this window and watching the sun set behind the Washington Monument. That's just not right." I shook my head and said, "It must have been done with mirrors," and the president laughed.

Wednesday, April 27, 1988 – *Great Friends*
Due to the state visit of the Canadian Prime Minister and Mrs. Brian Mulroney, I worked from 6:30 a.m. until 11 p.m. The Mulroneys got along better with the Reagans than any other head of state I've seen except maybe for Margaret Thatcher. Whenever the Mulroneys visited the White House, a lot of laughter and good times followed.

Thursday, April 28, 1988 – *A Vote of Confidence*
The Mulroneys were due at noon for a private lunch with the Reagans on the third floor in the Solarium. Before their arrival, President and Mrs. Reagan waited in the Diplomatic Reception Room. Mrs. Reagan would be traveling to the west coast the next day.

Gary and I stood about 10 feet from President and Mrs. Reagan waiting for the arrival while the president and first lady talked to each other in low voices.

NR: "Oh, I talked to the Wicks (longtime dear friends) and thought it would be nice for you to have dinner with them tomorrow night while I'm away."

RR: "Well, okay."

NR: "Would you like to go there or have them come here?"

RR: "Why don't they come here? That way, we don't have to have the entire entourage descending on them."

NR: "I thought it would give you a chance to get out of here."

RR: "Well, I kinda like it here."

At that point, Gary began to applaud. I thought, "What the heck is he doing interrupting a private conversation like that!?" President and Mrs. Reagan looked over at him and Gary said, "I take that as a vote of confidence." The president smiled and said, "Why sure," but the first lady glared at Gary turned away and continued her conversation.

NR: "I just thought it would be nice for you to get out for a change."

RR: "That's okay, honey. A place is a place, a table is a table, a meal is a meal."

Mrs. Reagan looked a bit exasperated as the motorcade arrived at the South Portico, and the Reagans then moved towards the door to greet the Mulroneys. I got the feeling the president was looking forward to having time alone the next night.

Is That All There Is?

Thursday, September 29, 1988 – *A Memorable Evening for All*

President and Mrs. Reagan were hosting a private black-tie dinner for France's President Mitterrand and his wife. About an hour before the guests arrived, the official gifts came over from the State Department—a large, heavy bronze horse sculpture and a linen table setting. I had them placed on a table near the doorway to the president's private residence study. Then I went back to the Ushers Office on the first floor to get the cards accompanying the gifts. When I returned to the second floor, I found President Reagan, wearing his tuxedo pants and an opened-collar ruffled shirt, looking closely at the bronze horses. Commenting on how nice the horses were, he said, "I suppose we could leave these out for the guests to see." I knew that Mrs. Reagan, with her eclectic tastes, would never go for that, so I suggested we check with her.

"Yes, let's ask Nancy," said the president.

I followed the president to find Mrs. Reagan in the beauty salon. Evidently, she had seen the gifts while I was downstairs retrieving the cards. She was already on the phone with Gary Walters, asking him to get rid of the gifts.

As she stepped out of the salon wearing a robe, her hair in curlers, I told her I'd get someone to move the gifts right away. She said with a smile, "Come on, Chris, *you* just take them." They weighed over a hundred pounds!

***

The guests, scheduled to arrive 6:45 p.m., would be escorted to the second-floor Yellow Oval Room for cocktails. President and Mrs. Mitterrand were due to arrive at 7. Dinner would be served at 7:30 in the private dining room, then all the guests would return to the Yellow Oval Room for the evening's entertainment.

The weather was cool enough for Mrs. Reagan to want a fire in the Yellow Oval Room fireplace—the first of the season. At 6:30, Ramsey, the butler, approached the fireplace and lit the finely stacked wood. But the fireplace damper was closed! Suddenly, the room filled with thick smoke, alarms went off, and Ramsey called the Ushers Office in sheer panic. Gary Walters, Dennis Freemeyer, and I came to the room in a heartbeat followed by Secret Service personnel and White House engineers. We immediately closed the doors to the Yellow Oval Room and opened the doors to the Truman Balcony at the opposite end of the room. To help get rid of the smoke, Gary told the engineers to reverse the airflow of the White House HVAC system. Then using fireplace tools, we hurriedly carried and threw smoldering logs off the Truman Balcony where they crashed below onto the south driveway. Fortunately, the Mitterrands were due to arrive via the north driveway.

Not since the War of 1812 had so much smoke been in the White House!

President and Mrs. Reagan were getting dressed and not aware of the situation. After 20 minutes of herculean efforts, the ushers, engineers, and butlers cleared the room of smoke. Still it smelled like a forest fire, so we placed large exhaust fans in the room, setting them to full speed which created a deafening hum.

Gary let Mrs. Reagan know we had "a small issue," but everything would be fine—except we wouldn't have a fire in the Yellow Oval Room that night. It was decided the guests would first gather in the main Cross Hall and then, after dinner, be escorted into the Yellow Oval Room.

***

Among my important duties that evening was wheeling around the after-dinner entertainer, the famous 1950s singer Peggy Lee, who was in a wheelchair. Over the years, Ms. Lee had become large and struggled with various medical issues. She wore a long, feathery white gown, and every few feet or so, the hem would get stuck in the front wheels of the wheelchair. It gave me a sense of what it may have been like for Elvis in his final months!

Earlier, my colleague Dennis had told me how much he hated Peggy Lee's hit song "Is That All There Is?" Because of that, he was glad I'd be rolling Ms. Lee around instead of him. I got an idea! I asked Ms. Lee if she'd be singing "Is That All There Is?" that evening. She smiled and said, "Why, of course." Then I learned it would be her last song of five on the program.

***

While the guests were enjoying dinner, we set up 36 chairs theater-style in the Yellow Oval Room. It seemed no scent lingered from the earlier smoke (or more likely I'd become used to it). At 9:20, the guests were seated and ready for the entertainment to start. I stood in the back of the room and listened to Peggy Lee croon. Then at the end of her fourth song, I slipped out to the main hallway to use the phone. I asked the admin operator to connect me to the Ushers Office. When Dennis picked up the phone, I said, "Dennis, get up here right away!" After the night's earlier events, I knew he'd arrive in a flash.

I walked back into the Yellow Oval Room as Peggy Lee was about to belt out the title line of "Is that all there is." That's when Dennis rushed into the room. He paused, at that moment realizing I'd set him up. Watching the priceless expression on his face, I had to go down on one knee fighting hard not to be heard laughing!

I thought Peggy Lee's song sounded good, although I had to wonder, "Is that all there is?"

***

But there *was* more that evening. After the performance, I brought the wheelchair to Ms. Lee while she was talking to President Reagan. She told him she couldn't imagine the United States without him. The president thanked her and said, "You just have to be sure and vote for who's going to carry on what we started," referring to the upcoming 1988 elections. She then asked, "What do you think of Dan Quayle (the newly named running mate of George Bush)? I can't believe he was picked."

The president looked a bit uncomfortable, then said, "You know, I've learned that three things become apparent as you get older. The first is you lose your memory, and I forget the other two." Then the president looked at me with a twinkle in his eye. I could see he

49

needed my help, so I gracefully turned Ms. Lee's wheelchair toward the door and made a quick exit.

Fall 1988

October 28, 1988 – *Saved are the Whales!*
The ushers were the one constant the president's senior staff could always rely on for delivering important messages to the commander in chief. These would often arrive via phone call or, in some cases, in-person via a senior administration official. Cabinet members, the vice president, press secretary, national security advisor, or even a member of the Joint Chiefs of Staff would come directly to the Ushers Office and ask us to deliver a message to the president. What follows is my transcript of a call I took for President Reagan from Press Secretary Marlin Fitzwater about the grey whales trapped in Alaska.

8:59 p.m.

Chris: "Ushers Office, Chris Emery."

Marlin: "Hi Chris. This is Marlin Fitzwater. How are you?"

Chris: "Great, how are you?"

Marlin: "Fine. Do you have a way of letting the president know that the whales are free?"

Chris: "*What* is free?"

Marlin: "Those whales in Alaska."

Chris: "Oh, great! Sure."

Marlin: "I know the president would like to know. Can you tell him?"

Chris: "Sure."

Marlin: "The joint effort with the Soviet ice breaker was successful in breaking up the ice and allowing the whales to swim free. We're going to release a statement using the president's name."

Chris: "I'll call him right now."

Marlin: "Okay, thanks a lot, Chris."

9:01 p.m.

Chris (to admin operator): "Hi, this is Chris. Can you ring the president, please?"

Operator: "Sure, Chris, just a minute . . . on the line."

Chris: "Mr. President, this is Chris in the Ushers Office. I've got good news. Marlin Fitzwater just called and he wanted you to know the whales are free."

President of the United State (POTUS): "The WHAT!?"

Chris: "The whales in Alaska are free."

POTUS: "Oh, good. *Good!*"

Chris: "Marlin said it was a joint effort with the Soviet ice breaker. It successfully broke up the ice and allowed the whales to swim free. Marlin said they are going to release a statement in your name, and he wanted you to know."

POTUS: "That is good news; thank you very much."

Chris: "Yes sir, you're welcome. Goodbye."

POTUS: "Bye, thank you."

***

The past couple of weeks, President Reagan seemed more relaxed—not that he ever appeared tense, but he seems to have become more easygoing. My guess is that with his administration winding down and George H. W. Bush doing well in the polls, President Reagan could ease up a bit. Reagan would be the first president since President Eisenhower who was given the chance to serve two terms. I guess he's counting the days until retirement. Well, a change of scenery might be a better description than retirement for him.

Those of us in the Ushers Office had been giving a lot of thought to the Bush family. All reports indicated the Bushes were warm, caring people. With their large family and all their grandchildren, we expect the White House would be busy with activities. Mrs. Bush always came across warmly on TV. By comparison, Mrs. Reagan was mostly distant, always having a million things on her mind.

I have to remember I'm a servant of sorts, but how wonderful it would be if the first lady and president showed a personal interest in us on occasion.

Tuesday, November 8, 1988 – *Election Day*
On Election Day, the Reagans hosted a private election dinner at 7:35 for 30 people. At 9:15, CBS declared George Bush the winner by a landslide, with the other networks soon to follow.

Wednesday, November 9, 1988 – *Victors Visit*
The Bushes and Quayles were due at the White House for a four o'clock ceremony. The couples arrived to greet a crowd of several thousand at Andrews Air Force Base and then boarded the motorcade headed for the White House.

Mrs. Reagan was expected at the Oval Office about 3:45 in the afternoon. Mrs. Reagan's Chief of Staff Jack Courtemanche came into the Ushers Office and asked me to call the first lady. "Hi, Mrs. Reagan, this is Chris." Before I could continue, she interrupted and said, "If Jack is there, send him up!" Upstairs he went while I headed to the Rose Garden.

By now, quite a contingent of staffers was clogging up the West Colonnade, so I made it to the far end where Secret Service Uniformed Division Sergeant Adkins was standing. I told him the first lady would be coming through momentarily and we should cut a path through the crowd. No sooner had I told him then I turned to head back to the Residence. There was Mrs. Reagan coming toward me, having just exited the Palm Room. The crowd parted, creating a path that made it easy for her to traverse. Mrs. Reagan smiled and said hello to several of the staffers as she walked by.

I got a good look as the motorcade pulled up to post C-9, just outside the Oval Office. President and Mrs. Reagan came down the path from the Oval Office to greet the Bushes and Quayles. Then they all headed back up the path and into the Oval Office for a few minutes. I moved up the Colonnade to try and get a better view, but it was very crowded. The Reagans, Bushes, and Quayles all came out of the Oval Office and stood on the steps of the Rose Garden. There was a two-tiered press platform in the Rose Garden and a camera cutaway in the NW corner. The darn cutaway was right in my view, so I could only listen as they all spoke.

Tuesday, November 22, 1988 – *Remembering JFK*

It was the 25th anniversary of President John F. Kennedy's assassination in 1963. Because so many of the Executive Residence staff had been working on that terrible day, I thought it would be fascinating to talk to them and ask what they remembered.

Assistant Usher Rex Scouten had been in the Oval Office supervising the installation of a new rug while the new drapes were being hung. Suddenly, someone came running down the hallway near the Oval Office yelling that President Kennedy had been shot.

At that moment, Butler Wilson Jerman had been in the pantry near the State Dining Room. No one could comprehend the horrible news; people were numb as they tried to busy themselves with work. Wilson said he had to stay at the White House all night and was worried about his six-year-old daughter, who was on a school trip to New York. She couldn't get back until after midnight because, as Wilson put it, "Everything just stopped; nothing was running."

Housekeeper Janet Bowen had heard the news from a painter on the ground floor of the White House. She immediately came up to the Ushers Office only to find the ushers unaware of what had happened. Immediately, the office television was turned on and remained that way for days!

Others at the White House that day were storekeeper Bill Hamilton and electricians Johnny Muffler and Bill Cliber. All of their reactions were similar—shock, then grief. No one left the building. Many staff members witnessed the president's casket being placed in the East Room at 4:24 Saturday morning. There it would remain under an honor guard for 24 hours before being moved to the Capitol rotunda to lie in state.

On Monday, November 25, 1963, more than 300,000 people, including dignitaries from over 90 countries, somberly attended the funeral of the 35th American president.

The Legend of Hang Dog

Thursday, December 22, 1988 – *Reagan White House Christmas Party*

The Christmas season was drawing to a close. The night's schedule included the final Reagan White House Christmas party, consisting of a private dinner on the second floor. I was working the day shift and Dennis Freemeyer worked nights. Since Gary Walters wasn't in due to his grandmother's death, I decided to stay and help with the dinner.

The first lady came down to the State Floor at 4:45 to greet Columnist George Will, due to arrive at any minute. The temperature on the State Floor was cool, even for me, which meant it must have felt frosty for Mrs. Reagan. Dennis and I went back and forth to call the engineers from the phone in the Ushers Office to crank up the heat ASAP. Funny, Mrs. Reagan would walk from room to room commenting on how cold it was, then she'd look at me and say, "These lights are too bright." I'd say, "I'll fix them." Then she'd go into the next room and ask, "Where do you turn these lights down?" With the light controls hidden behind panels made to blend in, the ushers knew exactly where to push and open the panel.

Christmas in the Reagan East Room, December 13, 1985 (Official White House Photo)

George Will arrived with his daughter at 4:50, and Mrs. Reagan walked them through the State Floor showing them the Christmas decorations. At 5:15, Mrs. Reagan bid farewell to them, and I escorted her back upstairs to the private residence. She told me she'd like to bring all the guests down after dinner to provide a tour of the decorations. "Chris, could you please have the fireplaces going?"

The guests began to arrive for the private dinner. Dennis took care of getting the guests to the private quarters, while I spent my time upstairs in the kitchen watching as the chefs and butlers worked. Dinner was served at 6 p.m. and once the dessert was served, I headed downstairs to make sure the engineers had the fireplaces burning in all the State Floor rooms.

When I entered the Ushers Office where Dennis was seated and Brian Rock, the evening engineer, was standing, Brian looked as white as a ghost. Dennis said, "Chris, you'd better sit down so I can tell you about the disaster that almost occurred." Dennis proceeded to tell the Hang Dog Story.

President and Mrs. Reagan with First Dog Rex. December 12, 1985 (Official White House photo)

Brian Rock was one of the few people on earth besides the president and first lady that Rex, the Reagans' dog, liked. The rest of us had, at one time or another, been bitten or snapped at by Rex. Brian would often take Rex for walks around the White House Grounds and usually had Rex with him when completing routine chores around the mansion.

This evening, as Brian walked off the service elevator with a cart full of firewood, he had an extendable leash hooked to his belt and Rex, the impossible mutt, hooked to the other end. Brian took a few steps forward as the elevator doors closed behind him. To his shock, he turned around to see that Rex had not followed him off the elevator. The elevator was headed down, so Brian made a frantic attempt to extend the leash. It wouldn't extend any farther, so he tried to cut it. No luck. He immediately dashed down the spiral service stairs adjacent to the elevator to the next level, the ground floor kitchen. Fortunately, Chief Florist Nancy Clarke had called the elevator. As the doors opened, there stood Rex precariously standing tip-toed on his hind legs. The leash was taut and about to hang him. Brian jumped in the elevator and disconnected the leash, rescuing poor Rex. And just in time. The elevator was being called to the basement level!

If it hadn't been for Nancy stopping the elevator, Rex would have, well, been hanged. What relief! The irony was we all hated Rex, the ole mutt. Hell, he'd just attacked me a few hours earlier while I was with the first lady.

As Brian left the Ushers Office, he tightly held Rex. Moments later, Secret Service Officer Gene Michinski stopped by. Gene had just finished his shift on post F10, which is directly above the Pantry where Brian had walked off the elevator leaving Rex behind. With sincere concern, Gene asked, "Boy, what was the matter with Brian Rock? I heard all this commotion and looked down the spiral stairs to see Brian flying down the steps yelling, "Oh f___! Oh f___! Oh f___!" Dennis and I burst out laughing.

***

Twenty minutes later, President and Mrs. Reagan escorted their dinner guests down the Grand Stairs to view the decorations. This time we were prepared. The lights were so low, I had to use a flashlight. The engineers had the State Floor uncomfortably warm with fires blazing in the Red, Blue, and Green Rooms, and in the State Dining Room. Everything looked beautiful.

The Reagans and their guests spent about 20 minutes walking through the State Floor. I could hear the president deliver a history lesson similar to White House Historian Bill Seale, author of *The President's House*. I stationed myself in a dark corner in the Grand Foyer while Dennis stood in the hallway by the Ushers Office and Woody the doorman was at the ready near the elevator.

I watched as President Reagan came out from the East Room followed by his niece Anne Peterson and her husband Jon Peterson, then Mrs. Reagan's brother Dr. Davis and his wife. The president was explaining the different ways the Grand Stairs had been adjusted over the centuries.

When they walked to the brass dates imbedded in the Grand Foyer floor, everyone asked what the dates were. I saw the president hesitate, so I stepped up (which the president appreciated) and explained the dates with a few tidbits of trivia. The president got ready to tell another story, so I stepped back to not be intrusive. Then the first lady appeared with actress Nancy Reynolds and two others.

Mrs. Reagan looked at me and asked what the dates in the floor meant. I smiled and told my stories again. This quickly turned into a trivia question-and-answer time. Someone would ask a question, I'd answer it, then the president would add something to it. Shortly after, everyone thanked me and said their goodbyes as they headed down the Grand Stairs.

***

Both Dennis and I decided to refrain from sharing the "hang dog" incident with the president and first lady; however, it has since become part of the White House folklore.

Friday, December 23, 1988 – *Tense Press Conference in the Rain*

At 9:55 a.m. on this rainy morning, the Reagans departed for California for the Christmas holidays. I waited at the end of the South Portico canopy as the president walked out so I could hold the umbrella for him. President Reagan looked at me with a glimmer in his eye and said (so no one else could hear), "It's great to be rich."

We then walked to the lectern. I held the umbrella for him as he gave remarks to the press regarding the recent Pan Am Flight 103 crash—or what became known as the Lockerbie bombing by Libyan nationals. After reading from a prepared statement, he was bombarded with questions from the reporters. Helen Thomas asked if the embassy was being notified of a possible terrorist act, yet the public wasn't told. Another member of the press yelled, "Do you care more for diplomats than private citizens!?"

With that question, I could hear the groans from my right where Presidential Chief of Staff Ken Duberstein stood with the first lady. President Reagan answered appropriately. As journalists Bill Plant and Sam Donaldson yelled out more questions, I handed the umbrella to the president, hoping he'd take it and walk away. That's what he did, but only *after* conscientiously answering the rest of their questions.

Portrait Unveiling

Tuesday, January 17, 1989 – *The Reagans' Portraits*

This night was the last dinner party for the Reagans—the portrait-unveiling dinner—which included the biggest group of stuffed shirts I've ever seen. I explained my thoughts to Gary Walters, who wholeheartedly agreed with my assessment. It included the highest levels of New York society: Mr. and Mrs. William Buckley, Mr. and Mrs. Charles Wick, Countess of Romanones, Robert Strauss, and Jerome Zipkin. Each guest was dressed to the nines and all seemed quite impressed with themselves.

Earlier in the afternoon, I had gone to Gary's office and got quite a shock when I saw President Reagan's brand new portrait. The president looked as if he were cowering, even frowning. My first reaction was he had news correspondent Sam Donaldson eyes! Donaldson, the man who haunted President Reagan for years, constantly yelling questions at every South Grounds departure, was now ingrained in this painting. How ironic! Honestly, I felt bad about this terrible and disappointing representation of our president.

During the dinner, I retrieved the portraits, which were covered with a thin white sheet, and put them in the Yellow Oval Room. After dinner, the guests slowly migrated to the hall outside the Yellow Oval.

The 40 guests were slow to get in the Yellow Oval and mingled outside on the room. Before long, President Reagan waved everyone into the room with my help and, a few moments later, yelled, "Be quiet!"

The first lady stood at the south end of the room in front of the portraits to the president's right. She began with a tribute to Aaron Shikler, the artist, and how he had done a portrait for the cover of *Time* magazine. I could see Shikler in the back of the room nervously leaning from one foot to the other, almost pacing. Known for his artistic talent, Shikler had painted the portraits of President and Mrs. Kennedy that hung in the White House.

61

The first lady then said, "We'll start with a portrait of the prez." Whoosh! Off came the white sheet, and everyone ooohhhhed and aaaahed. Then Mrs. Reagan stepped over and removed the sheet from her own portrait. A louder ooohhh followed. She went on to tell a story of how she did sittings for the portrait in New York at Gloria Vanderbilt's apartment. She described how Gloria, an artist herself, couldn't resist adding a final brush stroke to the first lady's foot on the Shikler portrait.

As the guests left, many commented on how they liked the first lady's portrait but not the president's. In fact, Nancy Reynolds, a close Reagan friend, came up to me and said, "Do me a favor? When the portrait leaves this room, HIDE IT!"

It was later agreed that artist Aaron Shikler would make changes to the president's portrait, which improved it considerably. This portrait can be found today on the State Floor of the White House.

A New White House Family

Thursday, January 19, 1989

The eve of the George H. W. Bush inauguration, I stayed overnight at the White House in the ushers' basement two-room suite. Chief Usher Gary Walters also stayed; he got the bedroom and I got the daybed in the adjacent sitting room. By this time in my White House career, I had already spent a half-dozen overnights, never sleeping very well. This particular night, my mind was wired thinking of all the events and duties scheduled for the days ahead.

On the final afternoon of the Reagan presidency, I was busy supervising the packing in the Oval Office. It was a strange scene seeing the Reagan staffers in the West Wing savoring their final hours. Gary Walters rolled Vice President Bush's chair from the Vice President's Office into its new place in the Oval Office. It replaced President Reagan's chair, which would be wrapped for shipping to his new office in Bel Air, California. I watched Kathy Osborne, President Reagan's secretary, tear up as she witnessed this un-ceremonial switching of the chairs.

***

Later that night, the Reagans' final White House dinner was private and low-key with only the president, first lady, and long-time friend and interior decorator Ted Graber. Dinner was served precisely at 7 p.m. in the second-floor Family Dining Room.

Beforehand, I went down to the Nixon wine cellar in the basement and found a single bottle of 1964 Dom Perignon. The temperature-controlled room in the mezzanine-level of the basement had been named for President Richard Nixon because he'd accumulated an incredible collection of fine wines and donated them to the White House when he left office in 1974. Only the ushers held keys to this room. Over the years, we'd occasionally add select wines, so the inventory remained at around 300 bottles. These included extra special wines, hence the '64 Perignon I selected for this special occasion.

During the dinner, I stood in the second-floor residence kitchen adjacent to the family dining room. When diner ended, the butlers brought in the dishes along with the not-quite-empty bottle of Dom Perignon. Ah! I so enjoyed the final glass!

***

The evening ended early as I got the signal buzz from the second floor indicating the president and first lady were going to bed earlier than I expected. I went up to the private residence and turned off all the lights about 10:10, I would be going to bed by 11p.m. Gary was sound asleep in the other room, but I was too keyed up, so I pulled the TV cart into my room. By 12:15 a.m., I had finished watching the movie *Wall Street* and turned out the light ready to sleep.

Friday, January 20, 1989 – *Inauguration Day*
Up at 5:55 a.m., I showered, shaved, dressed, and got to the Ushers Office by 6:20. At 9:30, President Reagan came down and walked to the Oval Office for his final time. As had become customary those last few days, a half-dozen photo ops with various staff occurred along his route to the Oval Office.

At 10 a.m., the entire residence staff gathered into the State Dining Room to bid a farewell to President and Mrs. Reagan. Gary presented them with a gift from the residence staff—a handmade wooden box the Carpenter Shop had crafted. Gary explained that the flag flying over the White House would be brought down exactly at noon when the new president would be sworn in. This flag would then be placed in the box for the Reagans to keep.

Next, President Reagan thanked everyone for their service. He joked that he'd never be able to find the light switches in their new home because for eight years he didn't worry about turning out the lights. When Mrs. Reagan spoke, she was emotional as she extended her thanks. Then they both waved and said goodbye as they left the room. I was disappointed they didn't take time to shake everyone's hand, but we had no time for disappointment.

The Reagans went out to the North Portico to greet the Bushes and the Quayles, who were arriving for the traditional tea.

Left to Right: President-elect and Barbara Bush, First Lady Nancy Reagan, President Reagan, Marilyn Quayle, Vice President-elect Dan Quayle. White House North Portico, January 20, 1989 (Official White House photo)

Tea was served in the Blue Room. After about 25 minutes, White House Curator Rex Scouten stood in the center hallway just outside the Blue Room door. As if on cue, Mrs. Reagan walked out and gave him a hug. She and Rex talked for almost five minutes, which was a bit awkward because all the guests remained in the Blue Room. Time was ticking.

Moments later, the guests walked out of the Blue Room into the Grand Foyer. There, Nancy Mitchell, Dennis Freemeyer, me, Skip Allen, and Worthington White all lined up to say our goodbyes. Wait a minute—Worthington White!? Why on earth was Budget Administrator Worthington White lined up to be the final staffer who would say goodbye to the Reagans? Heck, they hardly knew him!

Then Mrs. Quayle approached, and I walked her to the North Portico door. I turned to see Mrs. Reagan followed by the president approaching the ushers, so I pirouetted back to my place in line. Nancy Mitchell was receiving her hugs when I looked to my left and saw the Bushes looking back at us, waiting. Suddenly Mrs. Reagan was standing right in front of me with tears in her eyes. I reached out, and she hugged me and said, "Thank you for everything." Like an idiot, I only said "Thank you." What I meant to say was, "We'll miss you, good luck, God bless," or something more appropriate. Oh, well.

As the president shook my hand, I glanced to my left. The first lady had to be wondering, "Who is this giant of a man waiting to say goodbye?" It was Worthington! She hugged him, nonetheless. Gary did the final goodbye for our team. Then we followed the first couple out to the North Portico and waited for their motorcade. At 11:01 a.m., the limos departed, and we waved as they rolled toward the Northeast Gate to Pennsylvania Avenue. First was the president's limo, followed by the first lady's. As she rode by, she blew kisses to us, and off they went.

And so did we. The day's real work was about to start.

***

We had calculated we'd have until late afternoon to get the White House set up for our new family. The Inaugural Parade would wind down after 5 p.m., and at that point, President Bush and his family plus 29 houseguests would come into the White House. I was to work with Worthington White and the valets first task was to go across the street to Blair House and retrieve the new first family's luggage and clothing. Blair House, also known as the President's Guest House, had welcomed visiting heads of state for more than 100 years. Traditionally, it had served as the guest house for the incoming first family the night before the new president's inauguration.

This assignment proved to be a challenge. All the streets were blocked off; everything was tightly locked down for security purposes. However, by 11:40 a.m., our mission was accomplished, thanks (in part) to Worthington literally paving the way. We rolled several clothes racks across Pennsylvania Avenue and came in the northwest entrance of the White House.

We returned to the Executive Residence to see quite a sight. The entire staff—all 106 of us—were working fast and furiously. Beds had to be moved into rooms that never had beds before. Two huge moving trucks full of the Bushes' furniture were parked at the South Portico. I made dozens of trips to the second and third floors carrying luggage and clothes racks to the private areas. We could hear the swearing-in live on TVs throughout the Executive Residence. No one had time to watch, but we knew what was being said. At 2 p.m., I finally got to sit down in the Ushers Office for a few minutes. That's when a *New York Times* reporter called, asking questions about our activities. Quotes from that conversation appeared in the next day's paper.

***

The new president and first lady led the motorcade up Pennsylvania Avenue en route to the reviewing stand on the north side of the White House. The weather was partly cloudy with temperatures in the 40s—not bad for January. I watched on the TV in the Ushers Office as President and Mrs. Bush got out of the limo several times to walk the parade route for a block or two.

By 2:30 p.m., the Bush family and guests were seated in the reviewing stand in front of the White House. The butlers were ferrying hot chocolate and other food items. A few minutes later, a Secret Service agent told me one of the family members was walking up to the North Portico. I ran to the North Portico door in time to meet and greet the president's son, Neil Bush, and his adorable two-year-old son Pierce. Well, Pierce had had enough of the parade. He wanted a drink of water and then a nap.

Worthington dashed off to tell the butlers that a Bush family member was standing near the president's elevator waiting for a drink of water. Seconds later, Jim Selmon stood near the elevator with a silver tray and a tall crystal glass of water. What a sight! Jim stood six-foot four and Pierce was less than three feet tall. Jim leaned over to offer the little boy the glass of water. With no hesitation, Pierce took the glass with one hand and began to drink as Neil quickly knelt next to him to cradle the glass.

***

In the days leading up to the inauguration, I had been practicing saying, "President and Mrs. Bush. BUSH . . . President and Mrs. Bush . . . B-U-S-H." I didn't want to mistakenly refer to them as the Reagans. Still, Gary told me, "No matter how much you practice, you'll slip up. It always happens."

Pierce had finished drinking his water and Woodward (Woody) Willoughby, the doorman, opened the elevator for us. I pulled out my private residence reference map (aka cheat-sheet) to find the bedroom Neil and family had been assigned to. As we all stepped into the elevator, I looked up to the doorman at the controls and said, "Woody, this is Neil Reagan and his son Pierce."

Silence. Oh God, I did it! Neil laughed and queried, "Reagan!?" Ironically, a man named Neil Reagan *was* President Reagan's brother. We all laughed, and I felt like an idiot. Later, I learned that my slipup was a topic at the new first family's dinner conversation. Geesh, great start, Emery.

***

One by one, family members came strolling into the Executive Residence. I met Marvin Bush and his daughter Marshal, then took Marvin upstairs for a quick tour and came down as Jeb Bush and his son Jebby came in. "Where in the heck are the other ushers—Gary, Skip, Dennis, and Nancy?" I wondered. I was running ragged!

By late afternoon, I'd gone up in the Solarium to set up a computer for all the grandkids. I had missed President and Mrs. Bush when they walked into the White House. Minutes later, I was back in the Ushers Office to get a 30-second rest when a few items came in for the president's second-floor office in the private residence. So, up I went to the former Treaty Room. From there, I could hear President Bush speaking in the hallway as I was unpacking stationery and other items for his desk. I looked up in time to see him whisk by the door on his way to the Lincoln Bedroom. I finished unpacking and headed for there, too, catching President Bush as he headed back. So I held out my hand and said, "Hi, I'm Chris from the Ushers Office. How do you do, sir." He shook my hand and said, "Fine, thanks." After I explained I'd brought up items for his desk, he walked into his office to see them. I asked if he wanted me to put the items away or leave that for him to do later. He followed me to his desk and said, "Oh, this stuff is great." He opened some drawers and told me to put it "anywhere."

President Bush then opened several boxes of tiny lead soldiers and started placing them on the mantel above the fireplace. I helped as we arranged a few dozen soldiers representing various wars. Here I was, organizing armies with the president of the United States, unbelievable!

Then he stepped out of the room but stopped in the doorway and turned back to say, "Chris, there is one thing." As he looked at the thermostat on the wall, he asked, "How do you turn down the temperature?" "Oh, boy," I thought, "how do I tell the president our antiquated HVAC system doesn't allow him to adjust anything? The thermostats hadn't worked since President Truman!"

After trying to explain the thermostats, I told him I'd take care of the issue. In the future, he could call the Ushers Office and we'd get the engineers to lower the temperature. The president said, "I know Nancy Reagan liked it warm up here, but we like it a little cooler."

"We've already lowered it four degrees but could certainly lower it even more," I replied. He said 68 degrees might do it for him and the first lady. He thanked me by name and disappeared in a flash. What a warm guy, and he already knew my name. I was impressed!

***

Gary Walters, Rex Scouten, and I were walking on the ground floor hallway when the elevator suddenly opened. Four kids appeared from nowhere, yelling at the top of their lungs: "Bonsai!!!" Then they all jumped back into the elevator where a bewildered Woody the doorman stood at the controls. Up they went to who knows where.

By 6 p.m., the place had become quiet, too quiet. The calm before the next storm? Ten staff members sat exhausted in the Ushers Office: Chief Usher Gary Walters, Assistant Ushers Skip Allen and Dennis Freemeyer, Admin Usher Nancy Mitchell, Dink Chapman (electrician), Budget Director Worthington White, Roland Harley (doorman), Johnny Muffler (electrician since 1945), a Secret Service Uniformed Division officer, and me. Feeling slap-happy with fatigue, we laughed as we recounted our experiences from the day.

Johnny Muffler had joined the White House during the Roosevelt administration. He just shook his head, saying he'd never seen a family like this one—so many, so active, and so nice! He estimated that in the first six hours of the Bush presidency, the elevator got more use than in the entire eight years of the Reagan White House. The doormen were losing the battle.

We heard the elevator doors open. Out came six-year-old Barbara Bush, one of George W's twin daughters. She wanted to see the Flower Shop, so we asked Woody to take her there. Gary smiled as he picked up the direct phone line to the Flower Shop. When Nancy Clarke, head of the shop, answered, Gary said, "Barbara Bush is on her way down!" He quickly hung up. We all roared laughing, imagining poor Nancy, who was always on edge, dropping everything and scrambling to make things presentable for what she thought would be Barbara Bush, the new first lady.

At 7 p.m., everything seemed under control, so I headed home. I was due in early the next morning, Saturday. I left others to handle things, knowing they would have a late night waiting for the first family and guests to return from all the inaugural balls.

Saturday, January 21, 1989 – *Active Family and the Perfect Pass*
I arrived at 5:45 a.m. a few minutes later, the butlers notified me that the president and first lady had their morning coffee. When I reviewed the president and first lady's schedule, I saw they were due on the South Grounds at 8 a.m. for the White House Welcome Tour. At this official ceremony, the Marine Band would play music on the terrace outside the Green, Blue, and Red Rooms.

With the Marine Band's conductor Colonel John Bourgeois, I worked out that one of the ushers would signal him in time to play "Ruffles and Flourishes" followed by "Hail to the Chief" to announce President Bush's arrival. What happened next portended what this first family would be like to work with.

During the Reagan years, we had gotten complacent about the timing of events because, for eight straight years, everything went like clockwork. This morning, that all changed. President and Mrs. Bush came downstairs unexpectedly at 7:55. When they walked out to the South Grounds, half the members of the Marine Band were standing in the Green Room to thaw their frozen instruments. Mass bedlam followed as they rushed to get into place, and no one had the chance to signal Colonel Bourgeois about the president's arrival.

However, the Bushes handled everything with class, and no one felt bad. They greeted several of the eager tourists and then went up to the State Dining Room where they stood for 45 minutes shaking hands and greeting people. Feeling amazed myself to meet President and Mrs. Bush, I observed the tourists exiting the White House practically walking on air.

The remainder of the day, various Bush family members greeted the touring public as they walked through the White House, including the president's mother. The president's oldest son George W. also greeted many of the tourists on the ground floor. He'd say, "Hi, I'm George Bush. Nice to see you." One gentleman shook hands with George W. and thought he was meeting President George H. W. Bush, so he remarked, "My, you look so young!"

I had to go up to the private residence to deliver a message to Mrs. Bush and found the first lady and the president's mother looking out from the Queen's Bedroom window. They were waving as the tourists exited the North Portico. A large group was starting to mass, all looking up and waving back. Suddenly, the tourists began to sing "God Bless America"—a touching moment.

***

President Bush left the White House for a visit to the State Department. On his way back, he called the Ushers Office to say he wanted his entire family at the South Portico for his arrival. He asked me to get a sweater from his dresser, and he also said he wanted a football. Gary said he'd take care of notifying the family while I retrieved the president's sweater. Once I got it, I ran down to the South Portico.

Minutes later, the president's motorcade arrived. Several grandchildren were up on the South Portico terrace as his limo drove up the south driveway. I could see President Bush holding the car's PA microphone. Then we heard him announce, "Secret Service, please clear the balcony of those scoundrels!"

Next, President Bush got out of the limo and walked right up to me. "Chris, where's the horseshoe pit going to be put?"

I replied, "Where would you like it to go?"

The president looked exasperated. "No, you guys were supposed to have worked all that out with Laurie Firestone (his social secretary)." Then the president took the sweater I handed him, put it on, looked at his family, and said, "Let's take a walk." He'd invited members of the press who'd been part of the motorcade to come along, and they scrambled to join him. I went to the Secret Service phone at the South Portico Post C-11 and called the Ushers Office. Nancy answered, so I told her to get Gary down to the South Grounds ASAP. The president was asking me questions about the horseshoe pit that I couldn't answer.

***

Meanwhile, Gary had sent Worthington White to find a football. Worthington, the White House budget administrator, is a former Virginia Tech lineman and a big man. As eyewitnesses (a Secret Service agent and Worthington himself) later told me, here's what transpired.

The closest sporting goods store was on 13th Street, so Worthington started toward it in a half jog that quickly became a full run. He barreled out of the Northeast Gate and headed down Pennsylvania Avenue. He then burst into the sporting goods store in front of a line of customers at checkout and yelled, "I need a football, and I need it NOW!"

Everyone stopped and stared at this mad man. The store manager came up to him and Worthington exclaimed, "I need a football!" The manager said, "Well, um, what kind? We've got all sorts, we have—" Worthington interrupted the man. "Give me the best one you've got!"

The manager tried to explain that might be costly but Worthington, feeling the pressure of time, shouted, "I DON'T CARE WHAT IT COSTS. JUST GIVE IT TO ME!" The manager replied, "It's fifty-two dollars." Worthington grabbed the ball, slapped $55 on the counter, and bolted out the door like a lineman who'd just recovered a fumble. Everyone on the sidewalk steered clear of this apparent raving lunatic as he ran up Pennsylvania Avenue crossing against traffic, the football tightly cradled in his arm.

I was walking with the president's entourage when a perfectly spiraling arched football appeared in the sky. I followed it to where it had been launched and saw a red-faced Worthington in the follow-through of his passing motion. Before long, the president and his sons were playing catch on the South Lawn.

Sunday, January 22, 1989 – *Expect the Unexpected*

After only two days of this new first family, the ushers learned to be prepared for anything. I'd provided dozens of tours to various family members. At one point, I was showing Sharon Bush, the president's daughter-in-law and wife of Neil Bush, the roof terrace. She asked about the steep iron stairs and where they went. "Oh, that's to get on top of the roof," I answered.

Without hesitating, up she went. And she was nine months pregnant! As her White House escort, I didn't feel comfortable with this. But together, we walked on the roof all the way to the center flagpole and enjoyed the marvelous 60-degree weather.

***

Later that day, President Bush took a swim in the outdoor pool south of the Oval Office with his son Neil and grandson Pierce. Because he didn't have a bathing suit and had to swim naked, Pierce was upset. So, Neil evened it out and took off his bathing suit. I looked around for any female secret service agents. None! I then headed back to the Ushers Office.

That afternoon, the Bushes hosted a huge party for all their relatives and guests, totaling 450 people. As the president led a large group through his private residence for a tour, he stopped when he saw me and pointedly gave us ushers credit for the smooth move-in. "Those guys did it all."

An hour into the party, I was seated at my desk in the Ushers Office when George W. came in and asked where the White House admin operators were located. "I'd be happy to show you," I replied.

"Great. Let me get my brother, Marvin."

The three of us headed over to the Executive Office Building (EOB) via the West Wing. In the West Colonnade, both brothers remarked how they needed a break from the 450 relatives, most of whom they'd never met! As George W. put it, "We needed to get away from the thousand points of light!" Referring to his father's program.

As we walked through the West Wing, they marveled at the already up-to-date framed photos hanging on the walls. Each time they saw a picture of Chief of Staff John Sununu, they'd joke and say, "We don't want too many of him on the walls. Ya, we don't want a Sununu cult forming." They were joking about Sununu's popularity.

First stop was the White House Administration Operators Office in the dungeon of the EOB next door to the White House. The White House Operators were a group of wonderful ladies who were often (based on their location in the EOB basement) heard but not seen. When called upon, they could locate anyone anywhere to get an important call through. That day, the operators were delighted to meet the president's sons. The fact that two members of the first family were taking time to say hello and thank them for their service meant a great deal to them. I then took George and Marvin to meet officers at 058 (Secret Service Uniformed Division Command Center), where they were equally welcomed.

***

Early evening, the entire first family gathered in the East Wing Family Theater to watch the Super Bowl—or so we thought. Assistant Usher, Dennis Freemeyer walked into the Ushers Office looking bewildered. He told Gary and me he'd been standing in the private residence pantry hallway, thinking everyone was watching the Super Bowl in the Family Theater. The doors to the West Sitting Hall were open, and he could see all the way through into Mrs. Bush's study. There, to his surprise, he noticed a young woman, undressed, facing away from him. He realized it was the president's daughter Doro. So, he quickly ducked into the pantry, picked up the phone, and called the engineers, speaking loudly so she'd know she wasn't alone. Then he made a quick escape.

Gary, Dennis, and I were laughing about this as we headed to the first-floor service pantry to get our dinner. Natalie Wallace, the warm, wonderful, tough and never-shy pantry lady, looked up from her newspaper and snapped, "The way you fellas are carrying on, you'd think you saw some girl naked." We nearly rolled on the floor with laughter!

***

In late evening, Mrs. Bush called to ask about lighting a fire in the fireplace in their sitting room. When I inquired if she'd mentioned this to the butlers, she said she'd sent them home hours before. I said I'd bring up one of the engineers to be certain the fireplace was in working order. Just as I hung up, engineer Brian Rock walked in.

"C'mon, Brian. Mrs. Bush wants us to check a fireplace."

We got off the elevator on the second floor. As we crossed the main hallway, I could see President Bush in the West Sitting Hall talking to Mrs. Bush. He had a bad head cold and was wearing a blue-and-white-striped robe and a bright-yellow-billed Donald Duck hat!

As Brian and I walked toward the sitting room, I nodded to President and Mrs. Bush. Then Brian stuffed newspaper around the neatly arranged firewood in place. The Bushes walked in behind us, so I looked up and said, "Nice hat." The president responded by saying, "Aren't these great! The Halls (close family friends) picked them up at a Disney store in Virginia for the kids."

"I dare you to wear that hat to the Oval Office tomorrow," I said, smiling.

Mrs. Bush spoke before the president could answer. "Don't dare him, because he will!" He then put the goofy hat on my head and remarked, "It suits you fine." We all laughed.

I asked the president if he had seen the copy of the Lincoln White House floor plan I had left on his desk. He thought for a moment then said, "Oh, yes. That was really interesting." Mrs. Bush said, "I would like to see it, too. Where is it?" The president left and came back in a flash with the floor plan. He was looking at it intently when Mrs. Bush snatched it from his hands and examined it with fascination. I explained it was from Bill Seale's book *The President's House*. Mrs. Bush said she'd like to have a copy once things settle down.

By this time, Brian had a warm fire blazing in the fireplace. President and Mrs. Bush thanked us and off we went. A few minutes later, she headed down the back stairs to go for a walk on the South Grounds. About the same time, an envelope came over for the president's attention, so I took it up to him. This time, he was wearing the Goofy hat!

Walking out of his study with a smile, he said, "Where's that fire guy, Brian? Bar (his wife Barbara) was afraid he'd think I was crazy, so I wanted him to see my other hat."

Monday, January 23, 1989 – *A Morning Ritual*
President and Mrs. Bush turned out to be early risers, getting up by 6 a.m. or even earlier. The butlers would take in the morning's newspapers—*Washington Post, Washington Times, NY Times, Houston Chronicle, Wall Street Journal,* and *USA Today*—as well as bring two large cups of coffee, a glass of orange juice and saccharin for the president, a glass of grapefruit juice for Mrs. Bush.

I went upstairs with the doorman at 7:10 a.m. to wait for President Bush. When I opened the double doors, I could see him walking back and forth from his bathroom to his closet, getting dressed. He glanced over at me and said, "Good morning" then walked down the hall to his study to get his briefcase. On his way back, he looked up from reading his schedule and said to no one in particular, "I'm not having breakfast with the vice president." He was referring to the 7:15 item on his schedule.

At 7:20 as he got on the elevator, I said, "Sir, you have the most wonderful family." The president looked up from his schedule with a wry smile and said, "Well, if you still feel that way after last weekend, then they must be wonderful."

Tuesday, January 24, 1989 – *Mildred Kerr Bush and "My" President*

At 7:19 a.m., as President Bush stopped in the Ushers Office on his way to the Oval Office, he handed me a few handwritten notes. I was starting to like his style of communicating.

Later that morning, I got a chance to ask Mrs. Bush about their IBM personal computer and if she was using it. She said she'd started but never kept up with it. When I told her I was a computer specialist and would be happy to show her how to use it, she was delighted. As soon as things slowed down, she'd take me up on my offer, she said.

The big event of this day was the arrival of Mildred Kerr Bush, aka Millie, the first family's dog. I met the person who brought Millie, and as we walked around the South Grounds, Mrs. Bush joined us. Millie, a full-bred Springer Spaniel, was sweet and nothing like the Reagans' attack dog, a King Charles Spaniel. Typically, both breeds make wonderful pets.

As we got close to the Rose Garden, I heard a high shrill yelp—"YEEEEEOOOOW!" Stepping out from the Oval Office, the president called Millie's name. He immediately tossed her a tennis ball. Millie faithfully brought it back and the president leaned back and hurled it the full length of the Rose Garden.

Mrs. Bush then took Millie for a long walk on the South Grounds and invited me to go with her. I must say, getting to know the first lady was delightful—more than I'd imagined. I showed her the tennis court and I introduced her to Executive Groundskeeper Irv Williams. A wonderful man and a master at his craft, he'd been serving the White House since early in the Johnson administration—more than 25 years.

***

I kept thinking about a book by J. B. West, who was a White House usher from 1941 to 1967. In *Upstairs at the White House: My Life with the First Ladies*, he referred to President Truman as "his" president. J. B. meant that when he started at the White House, President Roosevelt had already lived there, but with Truman's arrival, he got to know the first family from the start.

Well, I believe President Bush is "my" president. Already I'd talked to President and Mrs. Bush more than I did the Reagans the entire two years I worked with them at the White House.

The Bushes are incredible, genuine people—so appreciative, considerate, and caring. Plus, I no longer had to dread going up to the second floor and fearing an attack from Rex, the Reagan's yappy dog who'd bite me.

I couldn't wait for the country to get to know and love our new president!

Tuesday February 28, 1989 – *Missing aspects of the Reagans*
Yes, I enjoyed getting to know this first family—so fun, grateful, and unassuming. But I did miss some aspects of being with the Reagans. For example, I liked their elegance and the almost royal aura they exhibited.

Don't get me wrong. I loved the Bushes, but key members of their staff, well, I wasn't sure of. I did miss Mrs. Reagan's Chief of Staff Jack Courtemanche, President Reagan's Appointments Secretary Jim Kuhn, and the president's secretary, Kathy Osborne. All wonderful individuals.

The Reagans had total confidence and trust in the Ushers Office and allowed us to do our jobs effectively. The Bushes (at this point) didn't quite yet have that level of confidence in us. They allowed their presidential aides to constantly interfere with our work, thereby driving us nuts!

Friday-Saturday, March 17-18, 1989 – *Pitter Patter of Little Feet—Lots of Little Feet*
Millie's puppies were born late Friday and early Saturday morning while I was on duty. On Friday at 6:30 p.m., 35 guests had arrived for dinner with a movie to follow—*New York Stories*. Mrs. Bush opted out of the movie so she could keep an eye on Millie. Tonight, was the night, she felt certain.

I was in the East Wing Theater when the phone rang at 9:09 p.m. President Bush, seated in the back row, reached behind him and answered it. When he hung up, he looked at me and said, "We just had our first puppy."

At 9:12 p.m., the president and I left the Theater. As we walked to the Residence, I asked if I should "scrub up" for surgery. President Bush laughed and said yes. Upon reaching the second floor, I waited as the president went into the Beauty Parlor, which had been transformed into the birthing room. Everything under control, at 9:20, we walked back to the Theater.

The movie ended at 10:20, and the president said goodnight to the guests without revealing any news about the puppies. At 11:15, I was ready to pack it in when the phone rang. The president asked, "Chris, do you have a cot or something we can put in this room for Bar? She'll be here all night with Millie and the puppies."

I called the Engineers Office and Clark Fries answered. "Meet me at the president's elevator immediately." As we met up, I asked Clark if he'd ever met President Bush? He said no, so I told him he was about to.

On the third floor, we found a single bed with a mattress and took it with sheets and all down to the second floor. When the doors to the elevator opened, there stood the president. I introduced Clark to him as we went into the Beauty Salon carrying the mattress. We placed it on the floor next to Millie's bed. After 10 minutes, the president excused himself and went to bed. About 45 minutes later, puppy number five was born. How amazing! I left at 12:10 a.m. and exactly two hours later, puppy number six was born. The count stayed at six, all healthy, all adorable. Although Millie seemed fine, Mrs. Bush was exhausted. Over the coming weeks, the puppies could be seen frolicking on the South Lawn, often with the president. I suspect he wanted to keep all of them, but eventually, they were given away to close friends and family.

It wouldn't be long, however, before the president partially got his wish. The pup they named Ranger had been given to son Marvin, who lived northern Virginia. Marvin would visit the White House often and bring Ranger with him. Over time, the president persuaded his son that Ranger needed the White House with its wonderful grounds. Although President Bush had no shortage of friends, the Ranger adoption reminded me of the quote attributed to President Harry S. Truman: "You want a friend in Washington? Get a dog."

***

The previous weekend, Marvin Bush had invited a friend to the Theater to watch the NCAA college basketball tournament on the big screen TV. I passed the president en route to the Theater from the Oval Office and asked if he and his guest wanted beer or soda. "Don't bother," he said, then ducked into the Doctor's Office and walked out with four or five soft drinks.

Shortly after, I told Alfredo, the butler, to take beer and popcorn to the Theater. Fifteen minutes later, Alfredo stopped by the Ushers Office and, in his heavy accent, told me what a good idea that was. "They were so happy that if I'd been a woman, they would have kissed me!" Now, that's happy.

Later that day, the president told me his son George W. had completed the purchase of the Texas Rangers, and I congratulated him on the news.

***

In the two years I was with the Reagans, I may have talked to President Reagan on the phone a total of five or six times. With George Bush, it was five or six times a day! He even called me to clear in a friend of Paula's, the Bushes' longtime live-in housekeeper.

The previous Sunday, President Bush called me from Camp David to say he'd like a light dinner because "I'm putting on too much weight." Our chef prepared a clear soup and salad. A few days after that, I asked Mrs. Bush, "When the president wants a light meal, is it only for him or for guests also?" She answered quite deliberately, "Everyone!" I then asked, "Was last Sunday's dinner too light?" She laughed and said it was fine. However, their guest, Treasury Secretary Nicholas Brady, told the president he was stopping at a restaurant on his way home for something to eat!

Minutes later I was talking to the president on the phone and again he requested a light meal. It gave me the chance to ask him if last Sunday's meal was too light. "It was fine, but Nick Brady didn't like it. But it was fine." The White House chefs with their extraordinary talent would come up with all sorts of variations of "lite meals" to keep the president happy.

Friday, April 28 - Sunday April 30, 1989 – *Broke the Mold*
This weekend I worked long days because the first family didn't go to Camp David. But as it turned out, a weekend with the Bushes in the White House was lots of fun.

On Saturday morning, their houseguests, Persian Prince and Princess Aga Kahn departed. On their way out, they spoke in French to one another. Being half French, I understood what they said. The princess remarked how much she enjoyed her stay and how great the Bushes were. "They broke the mold when they were born."

Later that day, a loud protest related to racism broke out in Lafayette Park. Mrs. Bush came down to walk Millie, so I joined her and told her what Princess Kahn had said. We got out to the South Grounds and could easily hear the protestors shouting. Mrs. Bush looked at me and said, "Racism. We're not for racism. Why are they protesting here?" I felt nervous because the crowd sounded unruly, but Mrs. Bush wasn't fazed a bit. She took her time walking and talking. I felt privileged to walk with her because Mrs. Bush trusted me to talk about anything from family to politics; she felt free expressing her opinion and asking mine.

On our way back to the second floor, Mrs. Bush stopped by the Ushers Office and glanced at the computer to see the log that kept track of their movements and events. This was strictly for the first family. I said, "It will be given to you when President Bush leaves office eight years from now." Mrs. Bush quickly corrected me and said, "Four years from now."

***

A few nights earlier, Mrs. Bush was swimming in the pool while the president tossed horseshoes. That's when she came face to

81

face with a rat in the water! President Bush came to her rescue. He took one of the pool poles that had a net, scooped up the rat, and drowned it.

Wednesday, May 3, 1989 – *A Glorious 20 Minutes!*
This week marked the completion of the first 100 days of the Bush presidency, but it seemed like a couple of years. I felt as if I'd known them forever.

We hosted numerous social functions, including three black-tie dinners in nine days. After the Bushes had left one of the black-tie dinners, they donned colorful NASCAR racing jackets over their formal wear and provided a pair of jackets to their houseguests; then everyone went to the South Grounds for a late-night stroll. As they crossed the ground floor hallway en route to the Diplomatic Reception Room, several departing dinner guests turned around and were surprised to see such a quick transformation in attire!

***

Earlier in the day, Mrs. Bush had planned a tea, so I went upstairs to ask if she was ready for the guests to come up. I found her sound asleep in the sitting room in the southwest corner of the second floor, so I woke her up and reminded her of the tea. She looked puzzled until she remembered, then she quickly stood up, smiled, and proclaimed, "That was a glorious twenty minutes."

Wednesday, May 17, 1989 – *Tennis Anyone?*
On Monday morning, Mrs. Bush had left for Kennebunkport, Maine, the family's summer home, and President Bush joined her the next day. While they were away, tennis star Chris Evert and her husband Andy Mill were houseguests, which was wonderful for me. Heck, when I was 13, I had a big crush on Chrissie! And she still looked great.

I greeted Chris and Andy at the South Portico and took them up to the Lincoln Bedroom. They were so nice, and I felt comfortable around them. After I gave them the history on their room, I made arrangements to get them lunch. Before I left, Andy asked, "Your name is Chris?"

"Yes."

"What should we call you?"

I quipped, "Your Lordship would be nice." They both laughed.

***

Fifteen minutes later, I was up in the president's private residence office tying the computer cables under a table. As I got up to leave, I ran into Andy, who was soon joined by Chris, and I gave them a White House tour. I told them President Nixon's favorite room was the Lincoln Sitting Room. During the final days of his presidency, in the heat of summer, he asked the ushers to have the air conditioning set as cold as it would go and then light a fire in the fireplace.

Toward the end of his presidency, on occasion President Nixon would drink brandy and smoke cigars, nod off, and drop his cigar, which would start a small fire, causing the smoke alarm to go off. The White House ushers, engineers, and Secret Service agents would respond by stomping on the smoldering carpet to put out the fire.

Chris and Andy found this story fascinating, but I told them not to tell anyone about it because I could get in trouble. She replied, "Don't worry. I know what you mean. One time at Wimbledon, I asked Princess Di where Prince Charles was. She said, 'He's such a baby, he'd never come to this.' I was so naïve. After she left, members of the press ran over to me and asked what she'd said. When I told them, they went crazy with the story. I felt so bad."

***

Wednesday turned out to be a crazy day. We were to hold a commemorative tree planting at 3 p.m., which was moved to the Diplomatic Reception Room. No, we didn't plant the tree in the room; the ceremony had to move indoors due to rain.

At 3:30, 260 members of the Senatorial Trust arrived for a reception. Shortly after, at 4:20, President Bush (back from Kennebunkport), Jeb and Marvin Bush, Chris Evert, and Pam Shriver were leaving for Capitol Hill to play tennis. We had been instructed that Marvin, Jeb, Chris, Andy, and Pam would be in the president's backup limo. Gary and I ran around like madmen getting them into the appropriate positions to get to the Congressional tennis courts. After all our work setting this up, the president walked out and sent his sons to the follow-up car so Pam, Chris, and Andy would ride with him.

When they returned from their tennis match against Marvin and Jeb, I asked Chris, "Who won?" She looked at me and, with a half-smile, snapped, "They did! No one told us they really knew how to play tennis!"

Later that night, the president invited his guests for a brisk walk "around the circle." Even though it was pouring down rain, everyone obliged. It was hilarious to see the Secret Service agents figuring out how to protect them all.

***

That evening, I received a message from the president's assistant, Patty Presock, that his uncle wanted the president to call him no matter how late. Uncle Lou Walker wanted to learn the tennis match results, so I mentioned this to President Bush on our way upstairs.

About an hour later, I reminded him again to call his uncle. He thanked me as he picked up the phone in the hallway. Nearby, the president's daughter Doro had been showing lengthy videos from her trip to South America, and the few guests who remained awake were watching them.

The president got Uncle Lou on the phone and said the boys won (6-2, 3-6, 6-3), then started to end the conversation. But at the last second, he thought of one more thing. Confirming his uncle was still there, he said, "Lou, did you hear the one about the blind man and the girl in the shower? Well, this girl is taking a shower when she hears a knock on the door. She asks, 'Who is it?' The man answers,

'Blind man,' so the girl doesn't bother to cover up. She opens the door. The man walks in and says, 'Wow, you have a nice figure. Where do you want me to install the blinds?' Lou, Lou? Okay, goodbye."

Thursday, June 29, 1989 – *Conversations at All Levels*

An off-the-record meeting was scheduled for the president's second-floor office in the afternoon. Secretary of State James Baker plus two others arrived at 2:55 p.m. I then escorted President Bush, General Brent Scowcroft, Senior Counsel David Bates, and Chief of Staff John Sununu up to the meeting room at 3:10. Baker left at 4 p.m., the others a bit later. When the president and his remaining guests came down at 4:28, they walked out to the South Portico. The two individuals who came with Baker got into their cars and left.

Later, at 7 p.m. Secretary Baker took Defense Secretary Dick Cheney up to the president's second-floor office, where they met with President Bush for about 15 minutes. Although I never did learn what these meetings were about, interestingly, I saw this type of activity just before Reagan ordered a military strike on Iran (although for those meetings, members of Congress also attended).

***

At 7:30 p.m., President and Mrs. Bush hosted a Cabinet dinner in the Rose Garden with 50 guests. It was absolutely beautiful. Two nights earlier, the Australian state dinner had been scheduled for outdoors, but the oppressive heat and humidity made it uncomfortable, so it was moved indoors. In fact, Mrs. Bush didn't hesitate to make decisions on such matters. She was good about making her thoughts known.

***

After the Cabinet dinner guests had all departed, Mrs. Bush came downstairs with Millie, and we walked to the South Grounds then around the "circle," as the Bushes referred to it. Mrs. Bush stated how great the staff was at the VP Residence, but they enjoyed the White House Residence staff even more. I told her our staff bent over

85

backwards to help them because of their appreciative ways. "Well, we haven't changed," Mrs. Bush responded.

***

The previous evening, the president had taken his 13-year-old grandson, George P., to the Orioles' baseball game in Baltimore. They left in the seventh inning with the score tied 1-1. Marine One landed on the South Grounds as the president walked into the Diplomatic Reception Room. There, I gave him an update on the ball game: still 1-1 in the eighth inning.

After escorting the president to the second floor, I got back to the Ushers Office where I had the game on the office TV, just in time to see Cal Ripken hit a home run. That made it 2-1. Five minutes later, the elevator was being called to the second floor. I jumped on and met the president. He had Millie and was holding a drink that could have been gin and tonic. With his free hand, he held a cane or walking stick. I updated him on the Orioles' score, and we talked about baseball as we walked around the "circle." He said he'd attend another Orioles game when his son's Texas Rangers came to town.

Funny, Mrs. Bush usually walks the South Drive circle clockwise while the president goes counterclockwise. As we walked from South Portico toward the Oval Office, we talked about rats and their abundance on the White House grounds, and I told the president about the infestation in the Treasury Building basement. Then, walking from the Southwest Gate across to the Southeast Gate, we talked about the dogs, Millie and Ranger. And from the Southeast Gate back to the South Portico, we talked about the infamous Rex Reagan, the Reagan's dog that had terrorized everyone on the staff.

***

Some of my early thoughts about this administration thus far: So many of the president's assistants (tons of them!) are young, which is just the opposite from those in Reagan's White House. I hoped all these aides and assistants and deputy assistants and aides to deputy assistants weren't just a bunch of glory seekers. A good assistant accomplishes, motivates, and takes on responsibility without demanding credit. This bunch seemed to be of the "me" generation, not caring about everyone as a whole and losing focus that they are there to serve the president and not themselves.

It's still early, I decided to take a "wait and see" stance.

Bulletin for President Bush

Late one Saturday afternoon, I was at my desk in the Ushers Office when I heard footsteps walking up the back stairs. I turned just as General Brent Scowcroft walked into my office. General Scowcroft was a retired U.S. Air Force lieutenant general who became the national security advisor to President Bush. He had held the same position under President Gerald Ford in the 1970s.

General Scowcroft was an unassuming, never-imposing, decent gentleman. He had become President Bush's close friend and trusted advisor. He walked into my office with a folder and asked if I'd take it upstairs to the president. I immediately stood as he handed it to me. When I started to walk away, he instructed, "Oh, and I need his signature."

I dashed up the back stairs to the private residence. I opened the door, then the second set of doors, and walked into the Cross Hall and listened to figure out the president's whereabouts. No one was in the West Sitting Hall, but as I walked, I could hear the sound of water running in the president's bathroom. I knocked on the door and President Bush answered.

"Yes?"

I partially opened the door. As I stepped in, I said to the president, who was in the shower, "Sir, I have an envelope from General Scowcroft. I'll leave it next to the sink."

"Chris, open it and tell me what it says," he responded. I'm thinking, "Oh no. This is marked Top Secret." I paused for a second and the president said, "Go ahead and read it." I read the two-line message that had to do with Beirut, Lebanon, and said, "Sir, there's a place for you to sign. I'll leave it right here." At this point, the shower door opened and out stepped the president. I'm thinking, "Do I hand him a pen or a towel?"

Then he stepped over to the vanity and opened a drawer to find a pen. He took the folder from me, initialed it, handed it back, and off I went. I got back to General Scowcroft and handed him the folder—making excuses for why it was wet!

***

Twenty-five years later, I was walking up 17th Street when I noticed an older man slightly ahead of me. I'm a fast walker and this old guy was keeping up with my pace! Impressive. Something about his gate was familiar, so I finally caught up and looked over at him. It was General Scowcroft! He had to have been in his late 80s.

"Hello, General Scowcroft. It's Chris Emery from the Ushers Office." We shook hands. I saw him smile as he recognized me.

"Where are you headed, General?"

"Up to K Street. I'm giving a talk to a group. How about you?

"I'm meeting my girlfriend for drinks," I answered.

"Can we change places?" he quipped. We both laughed and said our goodbyes.

Mr. Smooth

One day, President Bush asked me, "How many teams can the Ushers Office put together for our next horseshoe tournament?"

"Well, two," I replied.

"No, I want *good* teams. What about the rest of the staff?"

"You mean like the Carpenter Shop, Electric Shop . . . ?"

The president said, "Yes, let's go see them, and we can start with the Carpenter Shop." On the way, he stopped in the kitchen and the president, knowing that Executive Chef Hans wasn't the most communicative of people, said with a sly grin, "Let me ask Hans." The kitchen was full of chefs working. Off to the side, the president found Hans and went to talk to him. As we left, he leaned over to me and said, "I'm not sure Hans understood what I wanted." We both laughed.

We then cut through the Tradesman Hallway toward the Carpenter Shop. On the way back, the president stopped one of the butlers, George Hannie, coming out of the Storeroom. The president asked if George would put together a team for the White House Horseshoe Tournament. Hannie's expression was priceless!

To Chris Emery — May your life be full of ringers! Warm Regards, Gy Bush
9-14-89

The President and his brother Bucky recruiting Executive Residence A staff for the first-ever White House Horseshoe Tournament. L to R: USSS Agent, Bucky Bush, President Bush, author Chris Emery, butler George Hannie (Official White House photo)

That's how President Bush orchestrated the first annual White House Horseshoe Tournament. Teams were made up of butlers, chefs, ushers, and military aides as well as people from the Carpenter Shop, Grounds Office, Secret Service Uniformed Division, and Secret Service Presidential Protection Detail (agents)—a total of 16 teams. The president teamed up with his son Marvin, but they lost in the first round. Several hours after the defeat, I said to the president, "I understand condolences are in order." President Bush held out his hand to shake mine and answered with a smile, "Well, maybe I can still win the Sportsmanship Award."

From that exchange, I came up with the idea to make an award for President Bush. My boss Gary loved it. "Get the calligraphers to come up with something." We'd present it to the president at the horseshoe championship. They produced a black-and-red official-looking scroll-shaped framed certificate that said:

Mr. Congeniality SPORTSMANSHIP AWARD presented to:
Mr. Smooth, alias President Bush
First Annual White House Horseshoe Tournament

"Mr. Smooth" is what President Bush would call himself while pitching horseshoes. One afternoon, I walked over to the pit with Mrs. Bush when the president was playing. Toward the end of his match when points were urgently needed, he'd say during his windup, "Okay, here goes Mr. Smooth."

A few days later, the president, his aide Tim McBride, and long-time friend Don Rhodes got into the elevator headed up to the second floor. Someone mentioned horseshoes. That's when I turned toward President Bush and said, "I hear Mr. Smooth has become quite a legend around here." Don and Tim doubled over in laughter.

From Colombia to the Hunt for Red October

Tuesday, February 13, 1990 – *Horseshoes and Intrigue*

Mrs. Bush left for a literacy event in Salina, Kansas, at 9 a.m. and planned to be back later that night. The afternoon weather was exceptionally nice, so President Bush decided to play horseshoes. I received his call from the cabana near the horseshoe pit: "Chris, can you bring Millie over to the horseshoe pit? Marvin and Margaret (Marvin's wife) are bringing Ranger at about quarter of six. It would be nice for Millie to get out and play for a while."

"Yes, sir. I'm on my way," I replied. Then I went up to Paula's apartment on the third floor of the private residence. She was a sweet lady who had served the Bushes as housekeeper over the years. She did some sewing, some cleaning, and often took care of Millie. As I approached Paula's apartment, I could see Millie lying on the floor. After I knocked, I saw her move quite slowly as she woke up—Millie the dog, not Paula! (I'd been telling President and Mrs. Bush for months it seemed to me Millie had arthritis.)

Then I took Millie out to the horseshoe pit and watched as the president threw a couple of shoes. He asked me to direct Marvin and his family to the pit when they arrived. About 20 minutes later, Margaret Bush and their kids arrived sans Marvin. Woody, the doorman, took them up to the third floor, where Paula would be babysitting. I ran up to ask Margaret if the president was aware that Marvin wasn't coming. She replied, "Yes, I just talked to him." I tried not to stare, but Margaret looked beautiful. She wore a long black dress slit up the middle with a rhinestone sequence down the front and black lace stockings. She was beyond stunning.

She asked if I'd call her a cab and thanked me. Rushing around, she got her daughter Marshal into pajamas and made final touches to her makeup. I kept thinking, "Margaret looks fabulous. Could I ever let my wife go out by herself looking that good?" I then escorted Margaret to the South Portico where she left for her event, and I headed back to the horseshoe pit where the president was just finishing. We walked together back to the residence.

Wednesday, February 14, 1990 – *Family Concern*

George W. and Laura Bush arrived at the White House at 5 p.m. Mrs. Bush, who had gone to Bethesda Naval Hospital for an appointment, returned at 6 p.m. Margaret Bush arrived, and then the president joined everyone in the Diplomatic Reception Room. Afterward, they drove in a motorcade to the Peking Gourmet restaurant in Falls Church, where Marvin met them for dinner. By 8:45, everyone was back at the White House.

The president would be leaving at 9 p.m. for Andrews Air Force Base where he'd spend the night aboard Air Force One. Then he'd take off at 4 a.m. for a drug summit in Cartagena, Colombia. The purpose of the summit was to develop an agreement among Colombia, Peru, Bolivia, and the U.S. to fight the war on drugs. Mrs. Bush, George, Laura, Marvin, and Margaret had come to see the president off. I could sense their tenseness; his life had been threatened by the Medellín Drug Cartel, and everyone felt on edge.

Thursday, February 15, 1990 – *Safe Arrival Home*

Early in the morning, Mrs. Bush departed for a literacy event in New York City. For the remainder of the day, we watched CNN in the Ushers Office to follow the events at the drug summit in Cartagena. Fortunately, no incidents occurred, and the event concluded on schedule. Later, when Mrs. Bush came down to walk the dog, she saw me and smiled. "Well, I just talked to him, so I know everything is all right."

As we walked together on the South Grounds, Mrs. Bush told me that while she was in New York, the press had asked if she was worried about her husband's safety. She told them, "If I were worried, I would have never left the White House." She then laughed and told me the reason she went to New York was that she didn't want members of the press to realize how nervous she was!

***

The president returned to the White House aboard Marine One at 10:56 p.m. Mrs. Bush had come down at 10:45 so she could greet him. I walked with her through the East Wing Colonnade to get to the

South Grounds via the Jacqueline Kennedy East Garden, avoiding the members of the press who had gathered near the South Portico to cover the arrival. Mrs. Bush, Millie, and I stood under the canopy as Marine One landed. President Bush deplaned, walked up to Mrs. Bush, and gave her a big hug.

Once we were in the elevator, I could tell by looking at them the president and first lady were extremely relieved that all went well. I told the president how glad we were to have him back. He smiled, thanked me, and said, "It's good to be back."

Monday, February 19, 1990 – *Sneak Peak*

President and Mrs. Bush had spent the three-day Presidents Day holiday weekend in Kennebunkport, arriving home on the South Grounds aboard Marine One at 4:14 p.m. I was on duty. That evening, they had 47 guests for a dinner buffet followed by a movie, the unveiling of *The Hunt for Red October* starring Sean Connery and James Earl Jones. One guest was Tom Clancy, the author on whose novel the movie was based. Clancy seemed aloof, although maybe it was because he felt nervous in these surroundings.

The guests came in from the East Wing, up the Grand Stairs from the Ground Floor to the State Floor, then up the Grand Stairs from the State Floor to the Residence. As Tom Clancy and his wife reached the State Floor, I greeted them and said, smiling, "One more flight of stairs." Clancy looked at me through his tinted glasses and replied, "What? Is the elevator broken?"

I said, "No, this is the way all the guests are entering per Mrs. Bush's request." I should have said, "Look, bud, you can take the elevator and arrive alone on the second floor or take these stairs to where the president of the United States is waiting to greet you."

***

At 8:10, all the guests came down the Grand Stairs and headed to the East Wing Theater—49 people including President and Mrs. Bush. It was great to see a movie a full 10 days before its public release, especially *this* movie with its high expectations.

The Theater only has 51 seats, including the five extra brought in for this event that replaced the front row of oversized stuffed chairs. Once everyone was seated, including the majority of the joint chiefs, the president stood up, looked to Clancy, and said, "Tom, please tell us a little something about this movie."

Clancy stood nervously and said, "I hope it's good; enjoy the movie" and quickly sat down. Everyone laughed. Midway through the movie, I could tell everyone was enjoying it. In fact, I'd say it was better than good; the movie was excellent.

***

In the back of the Theater is a three-rung ladder leading into a projection booth. I climbed up the ladder and entered the booth to greet the evening's projectionist, Dink Chapman, a White House electrician. One of my favorite people, Dink and I had pulled off a few good pranks over the years. But this night, he was all business.

With two large projectors running, the booth's warmth was noticeable. Added to that, Dink was in a panic. One of the projector's take-up reels wasn't taking up! He was manually attempting to neatly pile the film as it flowed to the floor. He asked me to take over this task so he could queue up the second projector for the next reel.

Imagine how nervous the people at Paramount Studios felt lending the White House this movie before its release. In fact, they had reminded us several times of the value of these reels; they couldn't wait to get them back intact. If they only knew their valuable film was piling up in a growing mass of film spaghetti!

I was working hard to keep it from tangling, but the worst part? I was missing seeing the movie! So, I propped up on a small stool and watched it through the tiny projectionist window while continuing to harvest this multimillion-dollar cascade of film. Fortunately, because this was the second-to-last reel, this particular projector wouldn't be needed again that night.

At 10:25, the movie concluded, and the guests departed without ever knowing the potential crisis Dink and I had averted.

***

Another late night came to a successful end. With one of the ushers on a three-week vacation, I'd be changing from night to day shift the next day. That meant my sleep would be short-changed, as I was working late and starting at 5:45 a.m. the next morning. Then I would have seven days on the day shift and double shifts on the weekend. I'm not complaining—just describing some of the challenge's ushers face.

Because I loved my job, I enjoyed every minute I could be at the White House during those eight years.

Precarious Times

Friday, August 3, 1990 – *Star-Studded Marine One Departure*
I arrived at the Ushers Office at 5:55 a.m. knowing I'd be working a double shift. President Bush and the houseguests were due to leave for Camp David at 12:30 p.m. on Marine One; however, precarious events in the Middle East made everyone nervous. Iraq had just invaded Kuwait.

I walked with the president as he headed to the Oval Office at 7 a.m. He knew the situation in the Middle East was intensifying, with Iraq amassing troops in southern Kuwait for what could be an invasion into Saudi Arabia. I knew his day would be consumed with high-level meetings. As always, his mood was upbeat as he chit-chatted with me about baseball.

During that time, our maintenance team was replacing the floors in the State Dining Room and Old Family Dining Room, so I took a piece of old flooring and wrote on the back "Removed from State Dining Room 8-1-90, walked on by Presidents HST, DDE, JFK, LBJ, RMN, GRF, JEC, RWR, and GHWB." Later that day, I gave it to our White House guests Andy Mill and Chris Evert as they were preparing to leave with the president for Camp David.

At 3 p.m., I walked Chris and Andy down to the South Portico, then we headed toward the Oval Office. On our way over, we saw the great musician Eric Clapton, who had come to view the president's departure to Camp David. I remarked to Chris how good Clapton looked and that he must dye his hair. Chris leaned close and said, "Well, I dye my hair, too," and we laughed.

Chris and I were in a conversation when a senior assistant to the president came up and stood near me, obviously wanting to see Chris Evert. This guy who rarely acknowledges me patted me on the shoulder and said in an exaggerated, animated way, "Hey, how are you doing?" What a phony! Well, of course I did intros, and he started on how he just got back from South America setting up a trip for the president. Give me a break! While he was trying his hardest to impress Chris, I excused us, announcing she was expected in the Oval Office.

***

Chris Evert, Andy Mill and I arrived to the Oval Office where there was a lot of activity. Press Secretary Marlin Fitzwater, Chief of Staff John Sununu, Deputy Chief of Staff Andy Card, and General Brent Scowcroft were all present. Marine One had landed and shut down its engines, which only happens when the president has remarks to make.

I left Chris and Andy and went back to South Portico to join Eric Clapton, saying how, on my birthday a few days before, I was listening to my Yardbird albums. Clapton, a member of that band from 1963 to 1965, Clapton remarked in his heavy British accent, "That's going waaay back."

President Bush came outside and addressed the press, saying he condemned Iraq's actions and would insist its military get out of Kuwait. At 3:24, the president, Andy, and Chris boarded Marine One for Camp David.

Sunday, August 5, 1990 – *Lots on the President's Mind*
President Bush returned from Camp David at 3:07 p.m. When Marine One shut down, the president made a few remarks to the reporters gathered, then headed directly to the Oval Office for meetings.

At 4:45, a casually dressed General Colin Powell came into the Ushers Office. I had never before seen him out of uniform. I redirected him to the Oval Office to meet with the president. A few minutes later, back in my office, I answered the phone and the operator said, "Mr. Emery, the president is calling."

I quickly said, "This is Chris, sir."

"Chris, I would like dinner left out for me just like the other day, so everyone can go home tonight." With Mrs. Bush in Kennebunkport, he'd be dining alone.

"Yes, sir. I'll take care of it."

"Just like the other day," he said again, referring to having granola cereal, plain yogurt, and a small cheese platter. That night when he returned from his meetings, I told him dinner was all set. As he unbuttoned his shirt he said, "The Rangers are playing some ball."

I responded, "Yes, they're five games above .500." I stood in the doorway where he was undressing and added, "Their pitching is really strong, with Witt, Hough, Brown, and, of course, Ryan." I then backed out as the president headed to the second-floor kitchen.

"Sir, I'll take your masseur up to the third floor."

"Thanks, I'll be up in a minute," he said in good spirits. Amazing how he always seemed positive.

At 9:10 p.m., I escorted the masseur out and closed up. As I walked to my car, I looked up and saw the light on in the second-floor private kitchen. The curtains were drawn. I couldn't help but feel sad for the president eating alone. I imagined him rummaging around in that kitchen with all the world events on his mind.

Wednesday, August 8, 1990 – *U.S. Troops in Saudi Arabia*
I awoke to the news that the U.S. had landed troops in Saudi Arabia. Arriving at work by 5:35 a. m., I took General Scowcroft upstairs 40 minutes later. (Because he always took the stairs, we walked up to the second floor together and had a pleasant exchange.) As General Scowcroft waited in the hallway, I knocked on President Bush's bedroom door. No response. Then I knocked on the door outside his bathroom, and he came out wrapped in a towel. I said, "Sir, General Scowcroft is here to see you." The president looked over my shoulder, greeted the general, and thanked me. At 6:45, they headed together to the Oval Office. With the advent of Desert Shield on August 7 and the Iraqi move on August 8 to annex Kuwait, the president had to schedule early morning meetings with National Security Advisor Scowcroft.

***

At 9 a.m. with the press corps assembled, President Bush addressed the nation on the topic of Iraq's invasion of Kuwait. "At my direction, elements of the Eighty-Second Airborne Division as well as key units of the United States Air Force are arriving today to take up defensive positions in Saudi Arabia. . . ." At noon, he took questions in the press briefing room where he reiterated what he'd said earlier—that, at the Saudis' request, our country was sending troops and air power to Saudi Arabia to defend them from possible Iraqi aggressions. In August 1990, the president was focused on building a coalition of countries to produce a united front against Iraq. Congress and even the press approved of these measures. Later, on January 12, 1991, House Resolution 77 and Senate Resolution 2 would pass by overwhelming majorities, authorizing the president to use force against Iraq.

Sunday, September 16, 1990 – *Perfect Day for Tennis, But . . .*

My big chance. I was scheduled to play tennis against Presidential Assistant Fred McClure at 12:30 p.m. on the White House Tennis Court—something I'd wanted to do for years. I arrived at 12:06 and parked on West Exec Avenue. I was so excited! I walked down West Exec and over to B4, the Southwest Gate, and entered the South Grounds—the appropriate way for tennis players to enter the White House. Clear and in the low 70s, it was a perfect day for tennis!

As I walked to the court, I heard one of the groundskeepers, Dale Haney, calling me. He rode up on a utility vehicle and told me they'd been trying to reach me. Fred and I got bumped from the schedule so that Marvin Bush could play. *Rats!* So, I ended up taking a run for three miles with fellow usher Dennis Freemeyer.

I never again got a chance to play tennis at the White House, although I did play basketball a few times on the White House basketball court adjacent to the tennis court. That was the closest I ever got.

***

At 5:37 p.m., a tired-looking President Bush came back from the Oval Office with Mrs. Bush. He went straight to his upstairs office and turned on his giant multi-screen TV to watch the news. At 6:30 p.m., I walked up to his office to deliver an envelope with a paper that needed to be signed. As I entered, the president looked up and smiled.

At that point, I handed him the envelope stamped Top Secret and said people were waiting for his signature. I stood back a couple steps so I wouldn't see the confidential document. As he opened it, he said, "Oh, I've seen this." He signed it, put it in the envelope, gave it back to me with a fresh piece of tape on it, and off I went back to my office to hand the envelope to two Situation Room military staffers.

At 8:37 p.m., Mrs. Bush walked down the steps and stopped in at the doctor's office. She was there to retrieve her husband, who was receiving a neck rub. As they came out from the doctor's office, Millie and Ranger were lying on the carpet near the door. Once outside, President and Mrs. Bush talked in admiring terms about Paula, the nurse who'd just massaged the president's neck. They were both complimenting her—and deservedly so; she's a nice person. As President and Mrs. Bush stepped through the South Portico door ahead of me, I asked, "Sir, did you know that Paula is one of nineteen children in her family? When her parents had the fourteenth child, the state of Minnesota gave the family a TV set for having the most children. Then they had five more!"

"How incredible—nineteen kids!" But I doubted one of the facts as I retold this. "It might have been Michigan, not Minnesota," I said, correcting myself. Then the president stepped in with "Chris, it was Wisconsin." He knew better!

***

Next, the three of us walked past the stump of the little-leaf linden tree that had been planted in FDR's era. It had blown down in the previous night's severe storm. The president said, "I mentioned this tree to the Press Office today so you're likely to get some calls about it."

"I already have."

"Already?"

"Yes, sir. People in the Press Office called wanting to know the particulars."

"When was it during FDR's time, Chris?"

"It was originally planted at the White House in 1937 and planted at its current location in 1950," I told him. "You could get

Executive Groundskeeper Irv Williams to give you a walk around the grounds to learn the details about the trees."

"I have to avoid Irv. He might get me on the horseshoe pit and beat me in a game or two!"

***

As we approached the South Portico, Mrs. Bush said, "Let's go around one more time!"

"Are you sure, Bar?"

"Yes, because Pierre (the chef) feeds us too well."

The president looked at me and asked, "Chris, do you feel like walking around again?"

"I'd be happy to."

"I don't know. I think we're making Chris tired," he quipped. Mrs. Bush spoke up, saying, "You know, he does have to stay here until you go to bed, George."

"Well, I would've gone to bed already if it meant Chris could go home!" We laughed and walked around again. It was perhaps the longest and most enjoyable group of conversations we've had together. What an honor to be with the Bushes that day. I felt like their son.

***

After our walk while we were getting on the elevator, I said, "It looks like Millie's got something in her mouth." Whatever it was, I got it out and tossed it outside the elevator just as the doors were closing. After I said good night to the Bushes, I went down to the ground floor to retrieve that object. A group of Secret Service agents standing there gave me a hard time as I used a paper towel to pick up the decomposed remains of a rat. It had decomposed so much, all that was left were its toenails and a tail. Yuck!

***

Earlier in the day, Russ Appleyard, the Secret Service tour officer, introduced me to the Boston Red Sox's baseball pitching ace,

Roger Clemens. I welcomed Roger to the White House. Later when I saw the president, he bragged, "Hey, I met Roger Clemens today."

"So did I!"

"Where?"

"Here on the ground floor taking a tour." We both remarked on the bigness of this star athlete and President Bush concluded, "He's a good old Texas boy. Too bad the Rangers didn't hire him."

Gawking!

Friday October 5, 1990 – *Elegance and Beauty*

The Princess of Wales, Lady Diana, was coming to the White House for tea with Mrs. Bush. Now, I have met world leaders, celebrities, and the rich and famous from everywhere. Nevertheless, this day I would be paying particularly close attention; I believe the term is GAWKING!

With the imminent arrival of the beautiful princess, all the men on staff wanted to be a frog and be kissed by the princess! Sure enough, my boss Gary pulled rank and said *he* would greet the Princess of Wales at the North Portico as she arrived. I stood off in the distance in the main Cross Hall of the State Floor and watched as Gary and Mrs. Bush met Lady Di in the Grand Foyer. The princess was indeed stunning, even more beautiful than her TV and magazine images. I watched as the first lady and the princess ascended the Grand Stairs to the first family's private quarters on the second floor. I remember thinking, "What a magnificent aura this woman has—so elegant and purely beautiful."

Ninety minutes later, Mrs. Bush escorted Princess Diana back to the North Portico and bid farewell. Later, butler Buddy Carter who served them tea told me, "The princess was so incredibly beautiful, I couldn't believe it. Her legs were fantastic, and she wasn't wearing any hose. I almost spilled the tea!"

Barbara Bush greeting Diana, Princess of Wales, in the Grand Foyer of the White House, October 5, 1990 (Official White House photo)

Operation Desert Storm

Wednesday, January 16, 1991 – *Bombing Missions in Bagdad*

I was seated at my desk in the Ushers Office when CNN reported gunfire in Baghdad, Iraq, at 5:36 p.m. This soon escalated to bombings. CNN reporters Bernard Shaw and Peter Arnett described the scene as large flashes with explosions being heard. Starting at 4:30 p.m., fighter aircraft were launched from Saudi Arabia and off U.S. and British aircraft carriers in the Persian Gulf for bombing missions over Iraq. The entire evening would consist of the U.S.-led military coalition pounding targets in and around Baghdad.

President Bush addressed the nation at 9 p.m. As he walked in from the South Grounds shortly after, I told him, "Excellent speech, sir." He turned as if surprised and replied, "Why, thanks. It's not easy, but so far things look awfully good."

The Ushers Office immediately instituted 24-hour coverage. That meant each of the ushers would work 12-hour shifts, and I was first to take the overnight shift until 6 a.m.

At 1:33 a.m. on January 17, CNN was reporting new raids over Baghdad.

Friday, January 18, 1991– *Scud Missiles*

At 2:10 a.m., I was seated in the Ushers Office, having been at the White House since 2 p.m. the previous afternoon with only five hours of sleep in the last few days. I could go home when Skip Allen relieved me at 6:30 a.m. Gary had been at the White House eight more hours than I had. Although nothing happened between midnight and 4:30 a.m., we were there if needed. Tensions ran high.

A few hours earlier, Tel Aviv was attacked by a half-dozen scud missiles. Thus far, Israel had not retaliated. Meanwhile, the U.S. was in the process of "carpet bombing" Iraq and Kuwait from the air with B-52 bombers. Our ground troops reported skirmishes with the Iraqis along the Kuwaiti border.

***

The previous evening, President and Mrs. Bush hosted eight guests for cocktails, then the president called me about giving them a tour. As I approached the West Sitting Hall, Mrs. Bush asked, "Chris, do you mind showing them through?" She then said to her husband, "You go with them and I'll join you soon."

After we had completed viewing the Queen's Room, we headed back toward the West Sitting Hall when Alfredo, the butler, informed the president he had a phone call. Two minutes after I'd completed the tour and went back downstairs, at 7:05 p.m. CBS television reported that two scud missiles had exploded in Tel Aviv, Israel. At 7:30, the cocktail guests departed and at 7:35, the president, Mrs. Bush, and their son Marvin had their dinner.

At 8:14, Mrs. Bush and Marvin came down to the Diplomatic Reception Room and waited for the president. I went up to the second floor and waited with the elevator doors open. I saw him going back and forth from his closet area to his bathroom. At one point, he looked my way and said, "Hit the down button on the elevator." I replied, "It's already here, sir."

Seconds later, he came out, looked up, and said, "Oh Chris. Hi! I didn't know it was you standing there."

"That's because I was hiding."

He looked at me and said, "Things are getting complicated."

I nodded, and he went on. "Did you hear what's going on?"

"Yes, sir. I've been watching the media reports."

"How many scuds are they reporting?"

"Five to eight—and I'm continually monitoring all the networks."

***

Once we reached the ground floor, the president joined his wife and son to take a walk around the South Grounds. When they came back, he said, "I'm going to see Mary first (White House Nurse Jackson) and then deal with the scuds." Ever since the Iraq invasion of Kuwait, the president had been nagged with a sore neck this was a result from cocking his head to hold the phone between his shoulder and ear for extended periods. Moments after walking into the doctor's office, President Bush must have received word of a call he needed to take on his military secure line from his office upstairs. I caught up with him when the elevator automatically stopped on the first floor. When I jumped in, the president asked if I could move a massage table into the small room near the bedroom, so he'd be closer to the phone. As I brought the table in and was setting it up for him, I could hear him pick up the phone and ask for Defense Secretary Dick Cheney. Not long after, I heard him mention something about the "patriot"—referring to the Patriot long-range system to counter missiles and advanced aircraft.

At 3:20 a.m., I could hear the constant drum of a persistent protestor in Lafayette Park. This had been going on for days! It was 11:20 a.m. in Iraq and 10:20 a.m. in Israel. This hour's big headline was "Israel assessing damage, deciding whether to retaliate or not."

Monday, January 21, 1991 – *Who's Happy?*

This morning, I arrived at 5:45 a.m. feeling relaxed knowing President and Mrs. Bush were at Camp David. At 8:35, Mrs. Bush called to say the president had a touch of the flu and asked if I would request only soup for his lunch when they returned at noon.

Here are some of the highlights of the day:

11:59 a.m. Marine One landed on the South Grounds, President and Mrs. Bush, and Speaker Tom Foley and Mrs. Foley stepped off the chopper. The president stopped to tell members of the press how outraged he felt about the Iraqi threat to mistreat American and allied POWs by moving them to areas that were being targeted by the allied bombings.

12:02 p.m. In the Diplomatic Reception Room, President and Mrs. Bush bid farewell to the Foleys. Shortly thereafter, General Scowcroft told the president, "The weather is clear, so we should have a good night, and the Israelis are happy."

12:20 p.m. I wrote a note to President Bush telling him Chief of Staff John Sununu would come over at two o'clock and Bernard Shaw, the CNN anchor who had been trapped in Iraq during the initial U.S.-allied attack, would arrive at three o'clock.

2:33 p.m. I went down to greet Bernard Shaw, and he told me how CNN's reporting had aided in the tactical command for the U.S. Three minutes later, I escorted Mr. Shaw to the president's second-floor office. President Bush greeted him by saying, "How's the world traveler?" In the room were Bush, Sununu, Scowcroft, and White House Press Secretary Marlin Fitzwater. Shaw then announced to the group that, to report the conflict fairly, he could not take sides. It was obvious the president and his staff had difficulty with Shaw's statement. The meeting ended shortly thereafter.

Thursday, January 31, 1991 – *A Day Full of Tension*
    In the news: Iraqi troops gained control of Al Khafji inside the Saudi Arabian border.
    On this day, I thought I'd encounter delays getting into the White House due to the increased security for the president's State of the Union speech. However, I had no difficulty and arrived in the Ushers Office to relieve a grateful Skip Allen.
    Then I watched the president give his address on TV. He looked a bit haggard and, hard to believe, he needed a haircut! A good portion of his speech dealt with the war and was well received, with numerous interruptions for applause and standing ovations.
    At 10:10 p.m., W16 (Secret Service Agent HQ) called to say the president was en route to the White House, so I went down to the South Portico and waited. About a dozen West Wing staffers were waiting for his arrival. A large motorcade pulled up, President Bush got out, and he asked, "Is this a friendly protest?" They all cheered.

***

Once the president walked into the Diplomatic Reception Room, he conferred with General Scowcroft until Mrs. Bush, daughter, Doro Bush, and daughter-in-law, Margaret arrived. After a few minutes, the president ducked into the Map Room to have his makeup removed. I escorted Mrs. Bush, Doro, and Margaret upstairs, then came back and waited for the president. As he entered the elevator, I told him his speech was great, and he asked, "Oh, you watched it?" I responded, "Yes, sir. I wouldn't have missed it for the world." He thanked me.

At about 11 p.m., I took the press recap up to the president where he and Mrs. Bush were seated on the flowered sofa in the Sitting Room. He was wearing his worn-out blue-and-white-striped robe. As I crossed the hall, he yelled out, "What ya got, Chris?"

"The press results."

"Oh, thanks."

There was little new information in the press recap; it simply reported excerpts of what the president said.

Baseball's Greatest

Tuesday, July 9, 1991 –*The Splendid Splinter and Joltin' Joe*

On this typical late summer morning in Washington, I was working in my office when the president called, saying, "Chris, come on over to the Oval Office. I've got some friends I want you to meet."

"On my way, sir."

I arrived at the Oval Office and walked in. In front of the president's desk with their backs toward me were two men. They quickly stood and turned to meet me. Baseball Hall of Famers Ted Williams and Joe DiMaggio! Then President Bush said, "Chris, I know what a baseball fan you are, so I didn't think you'd mind giving these gentlemen a tour of the private residence. I've already alerted Bar (Mrs. Barbara Bush), so go on over."

Williams and DiMaggio were at the White House to attend an afternoon Rose Garden ceremony billed as a "Presidential Citation to Baseball" and these two greats were the guests of honor.

For the next 90 minutes, I walked with and talked to the two athletes many consider the greatest baseball players of all time. But while riding up in the elevator, all I could think of was asking Joe DiMaggio about his former wife, the bombshell actress Marilyn Monroe. I refrained, but I thought, "How inconceivable is this. Here is Joe DiMaggio riding in the elevator once used by a former president (Kennedy), who . . ." Well, that's not what this book is about!

Baseball's Greatest: President Bush honoring the Splendid Splinter and Joltin' Joe with a citation in the White House Rose Garden, July 9, 1991 (Official White House photo)

Timberwolf

Thursday, August 1, 1991 – *Whose Campaign?*

It was my 34th birthday. With President and Mrs. Bush returning from Moscow and not due back to the White House until 9:45 p.m., I decided to go for a run at dinnertime with Secret Service Uniformed Division Officer Donna Carpenter. Our run to the Lincoln Memorial and around the Mall was enjoyable. It was great to get out and even better to exercise with a friend. I was back in plenty of time to greet the president and first lady as Marine One landed on the South Grounds.

***

At 9:40 p.m., I went down to the Diplomatic Reception Room and waited for their arrival. I overheard Chief of Staff Andy Card and the president's son George W. discuss an upcoming meeting in which the president would "leak" the fact that he wasn't interested in running for office again. George W. said, "So, he'll probably announce this weekend that he's not running." Andy Card said something about the president wanting it leaked. George W. then started talking about the campaign organization. All this time, I'm wondering, "*Whose* campaign?"

As we all stood outside at the South Portico, the discussion turned to baseball. George W. told me about the new stadium being planned for the Rangers. The helicopter then appeared over the Mall and the three of us went indoors to avoid the hurricane force winds that the landing copter created. George W. commented on the chopper itself and how the Iraqi soldiers must have felt seeing American helicopters.

Once the helicopter landed, Don Rhodes let the dogs Millie and Ranger run out from the Diplomatic Reception Room toward President and Mrs. Bush as they stepped down from Marine One. When they approached the South Portico, the president saw me, smiled, and held out his hand.

"Welcome home, sir," I said.

As the president, Mrs. Bush, and Andy Card walked into the Diplomatic Reception Room, Card was telling them about the Hill and certain questions about the president's civil rights legislation. Again, I thought about the earlier conversation and wondered, "*Whose* campaign?"

While President and Mrs. Bush had both suggested it wasn't completely decided whether the president would run for a second term, evidently over time, his close advisors persuaded him to run for reelection.

September 4, 1991 – *Home from Vacation in Maine*

President and Mrs. Bush got back from their Kennebunkport vacation yesterday at 12:35 p.m. As they got off Marine One, he went directly to the Oval Office while Mrs. Bush came into the Executive Residence. As he walked toward the Oval Office, he looked over to the crew standing on the brand-new synthetic putting green just south of where he was walking. How amusing! The president kept looking at them, then back at the press corps who were at their normal arrival location. Should he go directly to the putting-green or not? Instead, he headed for the Oval Office. Mrs. Bush came up to the South Portico and, over the loud helicopter sounds, said, "Hi Chris!"

"Welcome home, Mrs. Bush."

She stopped and talked with her chief of staff in the Diplomatic Reception Room for a few moments, then walked to the elevator saying hello to the Secret Service officer and the doorman as she got on the elevator. I got on, we stopped on the State Floor so she could let Millie out on the North Grounds. She told me it had been the absolute best weather day they'd had in Maine, making it a perfect ending for their vacation. "What about Hurricane Bob?" I asked.

"It was exciting. They taped up everything and I stayed with friends while George 'escaped'." She was referring to the president's sudden trip back to the White House due to a Soviet coup attempt on August 19, 1991.

As we went up to the second floor, I mentioned how my daughter Katie had her first day of first grade today. Mrs. Bush responded, "I can remember my first day of first grade like it was yesterday. My mother took me, but I turned around and she was gone. I was terrified!" She asked how well Katie did.

"Well," I replied.

"Yeah, but she's used to it. She went to kindergarten!"

***

Downstairs in my office, I was updating the ushers' log when I heard over the police radio "Stand by all posts; Timberwolf South Grounds." Timberwolf was the president's Secret Service code name. I thought, "I bet President Bush is heading for the new putting green." I dashed out to the South Grounds. Sure enough, there he was talking to the workers who installed the green. I handed him a putter. The president smiled, but although he looked tanned, he didn't look rested, he looked tired, very tired. He also wasn't his jovial self. While he made sure the White House photographer got everyone in a group photo, he just wasn't the regular George Bush. He seemed preoccupied.

He putted a few times then tried a few pitch shots from across the driveway. After about 15 minutes, he told everyone he had to go to work after being on vacation, thanked them, and off he went. Later about two o'clock as I was preparing for Skip Allen to relieve me, I heard "Timberwolf and Scorecard South Grounds." President Bush was now at the putting green with Vice President Quayle!

***

I can't believe summer is over. With the Bushes gone for a month, time has flown by. Our projects went well: New windows in Mrs. Bush's office, two new windows in the president's office, and a new window in the Old Family Dining Room. The Oval Office repainted, with painting continuing on the South Portico. New floors in the basement mezzanine kitchen and in the first mezzanine pantry. West Exec Avenue repaved, putting green installed, and a new tennis court ready for the weekend. What accomplishments!

Saturday September 21, 1991 – *Stand By for the President*
President Bush phoned me from Camp David Saturday. A typical President of the United States (POTUS) conversation from Camp David (CD) went like this:

CD: "This is signal operator from Camp David. Could I have your name for our records, please."

Chris: "Chris Emery, E-M-E-R-Y"

CD: "Thank you. Hold for the president, please."

POTUS: "Hello, Chris?"

Chris: "Yes, sir, good morning."

POTUS: "Good morning. I don't know if Bar told you our plans."

Chris: "No, sir."

POTUS: "Well, we'll be coming back tomorrow at four o'clock, and there will be nine of us for dinner—our houseguest plus Secretary of State Baker, Mrs. Baker, and their daughter."

Chris: "Okay, great."

POTUS: "We'd like a light supper then a movie afterward."

Chris: "Alright."

POTUS: "Laurie (Firestone, Social Secretary) had some (movies) sent up here that we can have brought down."

Chris: "Yes, sir, we have several here now."

POTUS: "Good, something interesting, and for dinner something light. They made us something with artichokes, which was good."

Chris: "Yes, sir, I'll tell the chef."

POTUS: "Figure dinner at six-forty-five and movie at seven-thirty."

Chris: "Yes, sir, and also for your information, Neil Bush will be coming up tonight."

POTUS: "Oh great, is he there now?

Chris: "Yes, sir. He's upstairs."

POTUS: "Good, I'd like to talk to him. Have the admin operator connect him to me here in my Camp David Office after we get off the line."

Chris: "Yes, sir."

120

POTUS: "Thank you . . . goodbye."

Chris: "Goodbye, sir."

I called the operator, who told me Neil was currently on the phone with Mrs. Bush, so I told the signal operator to keep Neil on the line for the connection to the president.

November 28, 1991 – *A Sad Thanksgiving Brightened by a Special Call*

While the first family was at Camp David, I was free to enjoy Thanksgiving at home. We had just finished our dinner when the phone rang. The words I heard echoed in my head: "Roy is dead." Roy was my father.

The news came from my sister who lived near him in New Mexico. I was stunned; I'd talked to my father just a few days earlier. Although his voice was nearly gone due to laryngitis, he seemed in good spirits and even joked about air-expressing him a Maryland crab cake.

I couldn't believe it! WWII aviator, farmer, and lawyer—the man with the incredible intellect and keen sense of humor—gone.

I called my boss Gary Walters to say I'd needed to take off the next day. Gary sympathetically offered his condolences. Shortly after, the phone rang, and I answered. "Mr. Emery, this is the Camp David switchboard. Stand by. Mrs. Bush is calling."

Mrs. Bush: "Chris, I'm so sorry to hear about your father. Was his death expected?"

I thought, "How did Mrs. Bush find out?" I later learned Gary had immediately called President and Mrs. Bush to let them know.

Chris: "Yes, but no. It was still a surprise. He had been diagnosed with cancer and had recently come out here to Johns Hopkins for another opinion."

Mrs. Bush: "He was just here in DC?"

Chris: "Yes—he lives in New Mexico, but he came out the beginning of November."

Mrs. Bush: "How old was he?"

Chris: "Seventy."

Mrs. Bush: "Seventy! The president and I want you to know how sorry we are and that we are thinking of you. Wait a minute; he's right here."

POTUS: "Chris, I'm sorry about your father's passing."

Chris: "Thank you, sir. It certainly means a lot that you took time to call. Thank you very much."

POTUS: "You're welcome and we're so sorry."

I had tears in my eyes. "Imagine, President and Mrs. Bush took time out of their Thanksgiving holiday to call *me*."

The "FDR" Challenge

One evening while in the Ushers Office, I received a call from Mrs. Bush telling me they were in for the night, so I could go home. Because no doorman was on duty, I went up to conduct our shutdown activities. This involved turning off the lights on the second and third floors of the private residence (except for the president and first lady's bedroom area, which they would turn off when ready).

This night, I gave myself a challenge. In a small hidden closet near the top of the grand staircase was kept the "Gerald Ford" wheelchair. As had been widely publicized, former President Ford was an accomplished athlete who sometimes had mishaps, including falls. After one of his stumbles, President Ford needed to use a wheelchair but only in the confines of the private residence. However, the chair was kept at the White House in case future presidents or family members needed it.

Of course, President Franklin Roosevelt had the most use of a wheelchair because of his polio. That night, I had the bright idea to experience being like President Roosevelt wheeling around the private residence. I pulled the wheelchair out of the closet, sat in it, then wheeled into the middle of the hallway and peered all the way back toward the West Sitting Hall. I first wanted to be sure all was quiet and that President and Mrs. Bush had indeed gone to bed.

Then I wheeled up the ramp toward the East Sitting Hall. The floor was raised due to this portion of the second floor being above the East Room's extra-high ceiling. It wasn't easy getting a wheelchair up an incline, especially rolling on a plush carpet! "Roosevelt probably had a hardwood floor to deal with—much easier than this," I thought.

Once up the ramp, I took a right into the Lincoln Bedroom and turned off the lights, then wheeled to the Lincoln Sitting Room, and next across the hall to the Queen's Bedroom and Sitting Room. I was getting the hang of it!

As I wheeled back down the ramp, I was gaining speed, did a hard stop, and went into the president's office. Lights off. Then the

Yellow Oval Room. Done. Down the Cross Hall to the elevator and up to the third floor. Easy!

My progress on the third floor was going well until I faced my biggest challenge—the Solarium, the highest point in the White House. It was above the second-floor Yellow Oval Room, which was above the first-floor Blue Room, which was above the ground-floor Diplomatic Reception Room. This configuration of three elliptical rooms on top of one another was rare in American architecture. The Solarium had been added by President Truman, who followed FDR in office. Thus, it had likely never been scaled with a wheelchair. President Reagan had spent time recuperating from his assassination attempt in the Solarium. I've seen photos of him in a wheelchair there, although I'm sure someone had pushed him up the ramp.

I sat at the base looking up the 25 feet of what seemed like Mount Everest. I started maneuvering the wheelchair up the ramp, but I only made it a few feet. I backed down and tried with a rolling start. This time, I made it almost halfway, then no more.

But I wouldn't give up. I turned the wheelchair around and found I could make progress by going backward. With that technique, I conquered the Solarium!

After turning off the Solarium lights, rolling down almost resulted in disaster. My speed kept increasing and I sensed trouble. At the bottom of the ramp, I cut it hard to the left and went up on two wheels, almost toppling and just missed hitting a table!

"Okay, enough of this," I thought. It was time to get downstairs and put away the wheelchair. Back on the second floor, I sped like a pro down the Cross Hall when suddenly, behind me, I heard Mrs. Bush say, "Chris, what are you doing!?"

"Oh, uh . . . hi, Mrs. Bush. I was curious to know what it must have been like for FDR when he was in the White House." I could see Mrs. Bush was trying to suppress a laugh. Then she looked at me quite seriously and said, "Chris, go home!"

Vietnam Memorial

U.S. Navy Pilot George Bush in the cockpit of an Avenger (1942-1945) (George Bush Presidential Library and Museum)

Wednesday, November 11, 1992 – *A Memorable Memorial Event*

It was only one week and one day after President George H. W. Bush lost his reelection bid. I stood at the White House South Portico at 9:30 p.m. to greet President and Mrs. Bush as they came back from Union Station. They looked tired. We walked into the residence through the Diplomatic Reception Room to Cross Hall and got on the elevator for the ride up to their private quarters. The first lady said they had attended a party in which Senator Robert Dole and others paid tribute to President Bush, who quipped, "It was like a wake."

***

At 11 p.m., I was packing up and about to leave my office when the Secret Service agent nearby told me President Bush was about to come down and walk the dogs. I took the elevator to the second floor and waited for the president, who came out a minute later with the two dogs, Millie and Ranger. As he approached the elevator, I asked if I could walk the dogs for him. He said no thanks; he wanted to get some air.

Accompanied by a Secret Service agent, we rode the elevator to the ground floor. As we walked out onto the South Grounds, President Bush said he'd like to see the Vietnam Memorial that night, but he didn't want to upstage President-elect Bill Clinton on this Veteran's Day.

***

I stayed behind and watched as President Bush walked into the night, a Secret Service agent a few steps behind. They walked one lap around the south driveway then headed back toward the entrance. As they approached the South Portico where I stood, I heard President Bush tell the agent he wanted to visit the Vietnam Memorial around midnight without the press. The agent said something about bringing in extra agents. President Bush looked exasperated. "No, you don't have to do that. Look, what would you guys do if you had to take me to the hospital? You wouldn't wait to bring someone in. Check it out and call me. I'll wait to hear from you."

As the president and I walked back into the White House, we talked about visiting the Memorial. He said his heart felt for those who suffered from that war.

At 11:40 p.m. President and Mrs. Bush both came downstairs. I met them on the ground floor and, as the elevator doors opened, Mrs. Bush looked surprised to see me. "What are you still doing here!?" she exclaimed.

I responded, "What are you doing awake!?" She laughed and said she was asleep until a minute ago. She asked if I knew the president planned to visit the Vietnam Memorial. I said, "Why, no.

I've been totally focusing on all the work in my office." She rolled her eyes.

Then the president, Mrs. Bush, and their two dogs walked around the South Driveway where the presidential limousine had pulled up. They kept walking past the South Portico where I stood and had just started another lap when Mrs. Bush turned and brought Millie over. She asked the doorman to take the dog inside, then turned to me and asked, "Would you like to come with us?" I immediately responded, "I would love to!" Waving me along as she walked, she added, "We'll walk down here (toward the Southeast Gate) and the limo will meet us." She looked up to President Bush and said, "Pops! Chris is coming with us." That's when he asked the doorman to take Ranger (the other dog) inside. The three of us leisurely walked on the South Drive.

"Mr. President," I said, "I hate to dwell on this, but I've got to tell you how sad I am you'll be leaving the White House. I know you're hearing that from everyone around here, but my feeling is a bit selfish. I know you will be happier somewhere else in a few months, but I would rather have you here." The president responded, "Well, that's so nice, and such a nice way to put it. Thank you, Chris, and we're going to miss you all a lot."

***

Our motorcade exited the Southeast Gate and traveled south on East Exec Avenue, then made a right onto E Street. Mrs. Bush asked her husband about the press being present at the Memorial. President Bush said he didn't want any press people around; this had to be a low-key event. She said she thought he was required to tell them, but he clearly didn't want to discuss it, so I interjected, "All deals are off now."

After waiting for the red light, we made a left onto 17th Street. I was surprised we even stopped at the light, attributing the decision to not wanting to draw attention with lights and sirens. I was disappointed—NOT.

As we rode along, Mrs. Bush remarked, "I wonder what Marlin (Fitzwater, press secretary) will do after leaving the White

House?" The president said he was sure Marlin would be fine. Mrs. Bush added how much she liked him.

I was looking out the window as the limousine stopped at 17th and D streets. A delivery truck was next to us, and a man was loading something using a hand truck. I thought if he only looked over at us, he'd be amazed to see President and Mrs. Bush, but the man remained focused on his task. He probably figured we were just another limo in Washington, D.C.

The president said something about looking for houses in Houston. Mrs. Bush responded, "I saw Jack (Steel) on the tube today." (Jack Steel, an older gentleman with a wonderfully warm character and delightful personality, was one of President Bush's closest friends and a key advisor.) I added that I'd heard him on the radio. President Bush couldn't believe it. "Jack, on TV?" Mrs. Bush responded, "Yep, on the tube today."

As we continued to drive through light traffic, we talked about Mrs. Bush's laptop computer. I suggested she consider getting a fax board so she could receive faxes directly on her computer. She mentioned how Jeb (their son) was using Lexus software and how much his family enjoyed it. As the limo turned right onto Constitution, we discussed how internal faxes work. The president said to his wife, "Chris can set you up with a modem so our computers can talk." He then said he told Don Rhodes (close confidant and long-time friend) to computerize all the accounting, but Don looked at him in bewilderment. "Could that be done easily, Chris?" he asked me. "And do they have packages that can print checks?" I said yes to both, and Mrs. Bush seemed very interested.

When I mentioned that names on the Vietnam Wall were being read that night, the president said he wanted to read some at midnight and so did Mrs. Bush. But she immediately stated; it was more appropriate for her husband, the World War II veteran, to read the names, not her.

The Secret Service agent told the Bushes more than 100 people would be at the Memorial that night. The president replied, "You said there would be only fifty when you checked it out." Then under his breath he muttered, "I hope they didn't get word I was coming."

***

The limo turned left toward the Lincoln Memorial and did a U-turn, pulling up to the curb and stopping. Telling them it was my first time visiting the Memorial, they expressed surprise, saying how moving it can be.

After we hopped out, I let President and Mrs. Bush get a few steps in front of me so I wouldn't crowd them. He looked cool in his leather aviator jacket with the presidential seal while Mrs. Bush stayed warm in her black mid-length winter coat. The only light that night came from the moon—no press lights, no security cordon, no entourage—just an older couple strolling along. How amazing!

As they headed down the path toward the Wall, a passerby recognized the first couple and said hello. Walking farther, I was three steps behind President and Mrs. Bush when I saw him slap a rough-looking veteran on the back and say, "How ya doing? Thanks for what you did." Imagine the scene: this bearded vet wearing all denim was walking with his buddies in the opposite direction of a stranger who suddenly slapped him on the back. Looking annoyed, he didn't know the friendly slap came from the president of the United States. But by the time he'd walked past me, his face had lit up. With a sense of awe, he said to his companions, "Hey! That was the president!"

***

Meanwhile, President Bush was greeting surprised bystanders and saying, "Bar and I wanted to come out and pay our respects. It's almost midnight on the tenth anniversary of the Wall." As they approached the stage where people were reading names, several widows and family members of veterans came up and hugged them. One lady explained how she was about to read her husband's name and would be honored if the president read it instead. Both President and Mrs. Bush got up on stage. He read 10 or 12 names, then gracefully backed away as those in the crowd of about 300 applauded.

That night, I learned to appreciate the job of the Secret Service agents as they thoroughly checked all the people waiting to greet the president without being intrusive or annoying. President and Mrs. Bush shook hundreds of hands and signed dozens of autographs. At one point, a Park Police officer held a flashlight for Mrs. Bush to see as she signed autographs while a Secret Service agent held a small flashlight for President Bush. So many of the vets told him how much they appreciated him and how sorry they felt about him losing the election. A few even insulted the president-elect. With dignity, President Bush repeated how we all needed to rally around President-elect Clinton. I was so impressed at how President and Mrs. Bush were so patient and gracious, making each person they met feel special.

As we approached the end of the line of people, an older vet with a long beard and a tattered denim jacket that had military patches all over it wheeled up in his wheelchair. He was missing his legs. The vet asked President Bush to please sign the shoulder of his jacket. The president replied, "If you can move your beard just two inches, I can sign right here." Afterward, he called Mrs. Bush over to sign it, too. The vet said he'd treasure his jacket forever.

***

We finally made it back to the limo. Mrs. Bush got in first, then I did. The president had stopped to talk to a few more greeters, with the last one telling him he'd played horseshoes at the White House in July. After he got seated, President Bush mentioned how moved he felt by meeting all those people. One vet had even given the president a hat, which he wore the rest of the way home.

As we headed east on Constitution Avenue, Mrs. Bush said to her husband, "Tell Chris what Bob (Dole) said about you earlier in the evening." The president was busy checking out his new hat, so she said, "Never mind, I'll tell him. Senator Dole had such touching words, saying that Bush was a great president. And Dole was crying."

Lost in thought, President Bush reflected out loud, saying he hoped Desert Storm helped vindicate the Vietnam experience, and how bad he felt for those affected by the entire Vietnam episode. I saw a tear in his eye.

Autumn Change

Wednesday, November 18, 1992 – *Doing Introductions*
President Bush brought President-elect Bill Clinton over to the Executive Residence for a quick walk-through of the private residence. Both of the butlers, Ramsey and Buddy, were in the second-floor kitchen and President Bush was doing the introductions. Hearing Ramsey tell the story was funny, but then again, every time Ramsey told a story it was funny. He said how gracious President Clinton was and how he was impressed that the president-elect asked him how he was doing with genuine interest. Buddy added that it seemed like the president-elect had all the time in the world and was in no hurry to leave.

Thursday, November 19, 1992 – *Bad Day*
At 8:32 a.m., President Bush and his daughter Doro left for White Plains, New York, to check on his ailing 91-year-old mother.
President-elect Bill Clinton had visited the White House the previous day; this day would be Mrs. Clinton's turn. Arriving a minute before 3 p.m., she was greeted by Mrs. Bush. In front of the press corps stationed on the South Lawn, Mrs. Bush told Mrs. Clinton, "Watch out for members of the press. Be damned sure if they hear you, they will quote you." Mrs. Bush showed her around the third floor, then they enjoyed tea on the second floor. Later that day, Chief Usher Gary Walters gave Mrs. Clinton and three of her aides a more in-depth tour.
At 4 p.m., the president had returned to the White House, only to learn that his mother had died an hour later. The next morning while I was waiting for the president, I could overhear him and Mrs. Bush talking on the phone to the president's brother, Prescott, about funeral arrangements. When President Bush got on the elevator that evening, I told him I was sorry for his loss, and he said, "Thank you. When it rains, it pours."
"Yes, it has poured a lot this year."
He smiled and said, "You're right, Chris."

He then informed me they wanted a small funeral on Monday, and would I please discourage people on the White House staff from attending. He knew how well intentioned they were but wanted only family members present.

Friday, November 20, 1992 – The White House Taken Over by ABC-TV

Mrs. Bush left the White House before 9 a.m. to go to Georgia campaigning for the GOP senate candidate in a run-off election. On her way out, she said, "I can't believe after all this I'm going back out to campaign!"

At 1 p.m., President Bush left for Camp David. Then the mass of crew members, 240 of them, began arriving to set up the White House for the National Literacy Honors, which honors individuals for their leadership in literacy. The program included entertainment by Gerald McRaney, Delta Burke, Patti Austin, Reba McIntyre, Shannon Doherty, Naomi Judd, Eddie Van Halen, and others.

We had held this event two years before, again with the ABC-TV network setting up an elaborate stage and set. Once complete, it no more looked like the White House than the set from the Wizard of Oz! I thought, "For what ABC spent on this elaborate production, they could have taught every illiterate person in West Virginia to read!"

I also wondered, "When television networks are given the golden opportunity to set up in the White House, why do they create such elaborate sets that fail to accentuate the wonderful, ever-present, and historic beauty of the White House itself."

***

Sunday, November 22, 1992

President and Mrs. Bush both returned to the White House at 3:05 p.m. and went directly to the East Room for a quick rundown of the show. Later, they went to the Diplomatic Reception Room for a photo with the honorees and presenters. John, the young doorman, accidentally stopped on the first floor where I was standing, so I reminded him where the photo shoot was happening. When the president saw me, he said, "Hey, Chris, we need your help. Tell us what you know about these performers." I told him Patti Austin was a singer who'd performed here many times. Then sheepishly I confessed the only other one I knew was Eddie Van Halen. As the elevator doors began to close, the president sarcastically replied, "Thanks a lot!"

The guests began arriving at 4 p.m. Cal Ripken and his beautiful wife Kelly came with their darling three-year-old daughter, Rachel, whose birthday was that day. When the social secretary and the first lady's chief of staff saw Rachel, they went into a tizzy, saying, "I can't believe they brought a child!" I asked Gary Walters what the big deal was. He said, "It's very inappropriate to bring a child to a White House event."

"Why?"

"You wouldn't bring a child to a state dinner, would you?"

"THIS isn't a black-tie state dinner. It's a *literacy* event."

However, no one agreed with me. The first lady's chief of staff got Margaret Bush's babysitter to watch the little Ripken girl up in the third-floor Solarium. The first lady's chief of staff tole me, "We couldn't possibly allow a child. ABC has put up so much money for this, we can't risk it." I thought, "GIVE ME A BREAK. If a celebrity had shown up with a hooker in a thong bikini, I could maybe understand all the fuss, but what do I know?"

***

Three long days of setup for a one-hour show seemed unreasonable. But what bothered me most was that minutes before President and Mrs. Bush were announced, an ABC senior manager provided an overview of the program and then he profusely thanked the first lady's chief of staff for her wonderful help with the setup. I'm thinking, "I can't believe what I'm hearing." The first lady's chief of staff had been nowhere in sight the entire weekend; the only member of the first lady's office who appeared was a low-level staffer who came with a friend because they wanted to view the rehearsal. We, the Ushers Office, did ALL the work!

But that's okay. We're used to being overlooked. What irked me was knowing all the credit should have gone to Mrs. Bush, not her chief of staff! As part of the collective staff, we all serve at the pleasure of the president and first lady.

Thankfully, after all the work and aggravation, the show itself went smoothly.

***

After the show, the honorees and a few others were invited upstairs for cocktails with President and Mrs. Bush. I was asked to give a tour so I started in the Lincoln Bedroom. Then I asked Mrs. Bush, who was seated on the Lincoln bed, if she would introduce them to the Queen's Room, which she did well. As people entered the Queen's Room, George W. and Laura Bush arrived, the night's houseguests staying in the Lincoln Bedroom. After I introduced George W. to Cal Ripken, I stood by and listened to their conversation about baseball, new stadiums, and players they both knew.

I then showed the group the president's second-floor office and ended with a tour of the Yellow Oval Room. From there, President Bush guided everyone out on the Truman Balcony. Delta Burke came over to me and whispered, "Can I take those matches?" pointing to the President's House matches in the nearby ashtray. "Yes, as long as nobody sees you." She grabbed them and stuffed them in her bra! Later while people were leaving, she came up to me as if she were about to kiss me on the cheek and whispered, "Thanks for the matches!"

In the tour group was also actress and singer Naomi Judd. As we got on the elevator, I told her how much I liked her music. But stupid me. I thought this attractive lady was *Wynona* Judd, Naomi's daughter. I was thinking, "Wow, Wynona has lost a lot of weight." Much later, I realized she was Naomi, not Wynona. Oops!

Sunday, November 22, 1992 – *Got Through the Static*
While President and Mrs. Bush were at Camp David, the weather turned bad, so they had to motorcade to the town of Frederick

then take a chopper to the White House. During the motorcade, the president he called the Ushers Office. I picked up the military line and heard, "Mr. Emery, stand by for the president. Mr. President, this is Cactus. We have Mr. Emery on the line."

POTUS: "Chris, do you hear me? Over."

Chris: "Yes sir, I hear you." The static, though, was unbelievable. Was this a transmission coming from the moon!?

POTUS: "Please schedule Jeanne Flynn, the masseuse, for a six o'clock massage."

Chris: "Yes, sir."

I wasn't sure President Bush could hear my response and, after a lot more static, we got disconnected. I believed the poor-quality transmission was partly due to the scrambling of the signal, but come on; this was 1992, not 1942!

***

I connected a Compaq Contura Laptop PC in the second-floor pantry. It allowed the butlers to send me emails about what time dinner was served and other details. One email I received said the president wanted to know the Dallas Cowboys' score. By the time I answered, the butlers had logged off for the evening, so I went up to tell the president 16-10, Dallas over Phoenix. I found him in the West Sitting Hall with Neil Bush, George W. and his wife Laura, and Jeb Bush and wife his Colu (Columba). They all cheered the news.

Monday, December 7, 1992 – *Saturday Night Live Reenactment*

At 9:15 a.m., approximately 300 West Wing and Executive Residence staff members reported to the East Room. They were expecting President Bush at 9:30 that morning for an informal preview of White House decorations for the upcoming holiday season.

Days earlier, the president had worked out an elaborate hoax with houseguest and Saturday Night Live comedian, Bush impersonator, Dana Carvey, who would pose as President Bush. The Marine Band was queued to play Ruffles and Flourishes, Hail to the Chief. I swung the doors open and stood to the side as Dana Carvey entered to the roar of the gathering. At the podium, he did 15 minutes of hilarious President Bush impressions while President and Mrs. Bush stood in a nearby aisle enjoying the whole show.

Later, the president asked me to give Mr. and Mrs. Carvey a grand tour, which was marked by as many laughs as the event itself.

***

Mrs. Bush was busy upstairs in her small office, Room 214. I went in to place an envelope on her desk. As I turned to leave, she glared at me and said in a mean voice, "Get out of here!" She was kidding, of course, as she usually did whenever an usher would bring an envelope, because it usually meant more work for her to do.

Later while discussing computer needs with Mrs. Bush, she took out the ad for the IBM ThinkPad I'd given her. On it, she'd written, "See Chris Emery, Ushers Office for any questions." She told me she was entrusting me with her computer needs.

Friday, December 11, 1992 – *Christmas Present for Mrs. Bush*

President Bush headed to the Oval Office wearing an overcoat and a new cowboy hat. He looked at me funny after our good mornings and said, "What do you think of my Crocodile Dundee hat?"

I laughed. "It looks great!"

We walked to the South Portico together, then off he went after yelling for Ranger in his high-pitched yelp. Ranger came darting from the Rose Garden and caught up with the president as they walked clockwise around the South Grounds in the wind and rain.

Before lunch, I headed to the West Wing to talk with President Bush about getting an IBM ThinkPad for Mrs. Bush. I explained that, in my opinion, IBM had the best laptop available, but they were very hard to get. The president gave me the phone number of his friend and IBM Chairman, John Akers. He insisted he wanted to pay the regular price—wasn't looking for any breaks—but needed John's help in getting one for Mrs. Bush by Christmas.

Sunday, December 13, 1992 – *Magical "Christmas in Washington"*

At 2:11 p.m., President and Mrs. Bush returned from Camp David. Spike and Betsy Heminway—my absolute favorite friends of the Bushes—arrived shortly after 3 p.m. I found them lots of fun to be with, especially Mrs. Heminway. John, the doorman, and I got them settled into the Queen's Bedroom after Mrs. Heminway said it was her favorite. When I told Mrs. Bush, they were settling into the Queen's Bedroom, she said she thought they were to be on the third floor. Even though our notes were different, I wasn't about to tell Mrs. Bush she was mistaken. "Pops wanted them upstairs." As we walked toward the Queen's Bedroom, Mrs. Bush yelled inside, "Get out of that bed. We're moving you to the third floor!" The Heminways quickly came out hugging and saying their hellos. Mrs. Bush explained someone else would be staying in the Queen's Bedroom—someone more important, she jokingly added.

"Who?" the Heminways asked.

"The Lays."

"Who are they? They don't sound important."

Everyone was still laughing as we climbed the back stairs to Room 327.

That evening, the Bushes and their guests went to the "Christmas in Washington" taping at the Pension Building. The president phoned me from there and asked that I retrieve his black briefcase and some presidential golf balls. So, I went to the Oval Office and rifled through several drawers. Finally, I found the golf balls and the president's briefcase.

President Bush often asked me to go to the Oval Office to retrieve a briefcase or papers. As for the golf balls, he always had some on hand. Whenever he got the chance, he'd step outside to the putting green and practice.

***

The Bushes invited several of the "Christmas in Washington" guests back to the White House for dinner. The entourage first went up to the second floor, then down to the State Floor to view the

Christmas decorations. At 8 p.m., they all went back up where they waited for Neil Diamond, Julie Andrews, and George Stevens. I loved these private dinners, especially on a Sunday because they were very relaxing, as compared to events run by the president's social secretary, which always tended to have more of a frantic flair.

The beautiful Julie Andrews arrived and, at age 57, looked 37! Wow! I imagine any male my age fell in love with her after she starred in *The Sound of Music*. On this evening, she looked stunning and was warm and friendly. The legendary singer Neil Diamond was a bit reserved, while film director George Stevens and his wife were engaging and fun to be around.

***

After dinner at 9:30 p.m., everyone came down the Grand Staircase. Earlier, the president told me he'd ask Neil Diamond to play the piano. Sure enough, after a brief tour, they gathered around the Steinway piano just outside the Ushers Office. Everyone listened as I shared the historic trivia that nine presidents had played this piano, starting with FDR.

With that, President Bush stretched his fingers, stepped over to the bench, and in an exaggerated manner flipped up the back of his suit coat, and sat down at the keyboard. Everyone was laughing as he played "Suwanee River" with four fingers. Then Neil Diamond sat down to play and, with Julie Andrews, led everyone in singing White Christmas. Chef Pierre Chambrin, pastry chef Roland Mesnier, and electrician Jeff Freeburger all joined in!

Everyone had such a good time. Later, as Julie Andrews' car pulled away from the South Portico, I leaned close to Mrs. Bush and told her I was encouraging Chef Pierre to tell Julie Andrews he was one of the Von Trappe children (based on the family chronicled in *The Sound of Music*)! She burst out laughing, then looked at me seriously and said, "I'd believe it."

Escorting Mrs. Bush to the second floor, we arrived to find Neil Diamond music blaring out of the stereo and Mrs. Heminway dancing. Before long, Mrs. Bush was doing the twist along with her.

***

Later, President Bush, Mrs. Bush, and the houseguests all came downstairs to take a walk. I heard them laughing as they walked through the Diplomatic Reception Room. I went outside with them but waited at the South Portico to give the couples their space. After walking the "circle," they went into the Oval Office and, 15 minutes later, came back in through the Diplomatic Reception Room. The three men were well ahead of the ladies and talked in a serious mood about what the president would do in private life. I heard the president say, "I need to do something that'll make some money—not a lot, just some."

***

Before I left the White House for the night, I ran over to the Oval Office and stuck this hideous three-foot fisherman figurine on the chair next to the president's desk. I knew the president absolutely hated it. It was something which the White House Gift Unit had received. Mrs. Bush's aide, Peggy Swift, brought it over weeks earlier, and we've been sticking him in various places all around the White House.

I laughed so hard this night my side hurt!

Tuesday, December 15, 1992 – *Tentative Times of Change*
I couldn't sleep thinking of the impending changes coming with the new president and first lady. I felt anxious, worried, and sad all at the same time. In fact, I had the scary thought that I could lose my job.

January 20th was only a few days after my seventh White House anniversary.

Friday, December 25, 1992 – *Merry Christmas and a Missing Present*
As has been the custom since they moved to the White House, the first family stayed at Camp David for Christmas, so I was able to enjoy Christmas with my family at my home in Maryland. My

daughter and my three stepchildren were happy I could enjoy a quiet day off.

However, at 9:30 a.m., I received a call. "This is the Camp David operator. The president is calling for you. Could we please have your location for our records?"

I answered, "Laurel, Maryland."

"Thank you. Stand by."

I waited for 30 or so seconds, then heard the voice of Don Rhodes, confidant and close friend of the president. "Chris, where's the present for Mrs. Bush from the president? I gave you the check for it. Where is it?" Don was referring to the IBM laptop I had worked to get from IBM and configured for Mrs. Bush's use.

I explained how the valet, Orlando, had taken it up to Camp David the day before. "It must be there somewhere."

Don said, "I'll find Orlando, then call you back."

Don had explained they were only halfway through opening all the presents. So, I called the White House housekeeper, the sensationally competent Chris Limerick. Chris described how she had wrapped the gift. With these details, I called Camp David and relayed to Don that the missing gift was a silver-wrapped box with red ribbon placed inside a plain box to protect the ribbon. Don called me 20 minutes later to say Orlando had located the box and all was fine. Whew!

***

At 12:15 p.m., I received a call from Mrs. Bush who was elated with the gift, her IBM ThinkPad. She wanted to know how to load her files from the Grid laptop she was currently using. As I told her, she wrote it all down. She even commented, "I can't believe I'm ruining your Christmas with this." I assured her she wasn't ruining anything. Really, I was delighted to help.

I explained to her how to copy her files. After we hung up, I thought about something else I needed to tell her. So I called back, first dialing the White House operator. I identified myself, then asked for Camp David. They switched me to the military signal operator.

After a few moments, I heard, "Hi, Chris, Merry Christmas." Wow, it was the president himself.

"Merry Christmas, sir."

"She's right here."

I then explained the updated instructions to Mrs. Bush who wrote them down again, thanked me, and wished my family and me a Merry Christmas.

Sunday when they returned from Camp David, I was at the White House to greet them. Carrying her IBM ThinkPad in its carrying case, Mrs. Bush told me how much she loved it. She said that as soon as she opened this present, she disappeared so she could go and use it.

Yes, the president had told me that would happen!

New Energy

Wednesday, January 20, 1993 – *Inauguration Day*

Melancholy replaced by nervous anticipation were the emotions experienced by the Executive Residence staff as we bid farewell to the departing first family and then worked feverishly to prepare for the arrival of the new first family. President George H. W. Bush and First Lady Barbara Bush had become so close to everyone on staff, their departure made us realize how quickly the four years went by.

This transition was unlike four years ago when the Reagans departed. With George H. W. Bush having been vice president for eight years, the Executive Residence staff was familiar with the Bushes and had a good idea what to expect, which made for a smooth transition.

*** *** ***

The inaugural morning was partly sunny with temperatures in the upper 30s—not bad for January. At 10:10 a.m., the entire Executive Residence staff stood in a large semicircle in the State Dining Room as President and Mrs. Bush entered. The president fought back tears as they walked around the room greeting each member of the staff. With the president too emotional to speak, he stood next to a smiling Mrs. Bush who thanked everyone. As the Bushes left the room, the staff quickly moved to their assigned areas throughout the mansion to start the work that wouldn't end till late in the day.

At 10:35 a.m., President and Mrs. Bush were joined by Vice President and Mrs. Quayle as they walked out to the North Portico to greet President-elect and Mrs. Clinton, and Vice President-elect and Mrs. Gore upon their arrival. The ushers stood by just inside the Grand Foyer.

President and Mrs. Bush greeting President-elect Clinton and family, January 20, 1993 (Official White house photograph)

The motorcade arrived and, after greetings, Mrs. Bush followed by President Bush led everyone into the Grand Foyer where she introduced me to President-elect Clinton. We shook hands; he was pleasant although distracted and understandably so.

Next was the traditional tea in the Blue Room. I stood by in the main Cross Hall outside of the Blue Room when President Bush's appointment secretary Tim McBride approached and handed me an envelope addressed to "Linda Bloodworth Thomason, Lincoln Bedroom." Linda and Harry Thomason from Hollywood were close friends of the Clintons. Tim said that President Bush had reviewed its contents and thought it would be okay, so I slipped the envelope into my suit pocket.

Later, I looked inside the envelope. A letter read, *"Dear Linda, I hope you enjoy your stay in the Lincoln Bedroom. Just remember, I was here first, and I'll be back. I enjoyed your show. Rush Limbaugh."* Rush Limbaugh, a controversial conservative radio talk-show host, had been an overnight guest of the Bushes a few months earlier and had stayed in the Lincoln Bedroom. The

Thomasons ended up staying in the Lincoln Bedroom the next night; I left the letter in their room. Later, when Harry Thomason had an address at the National Press Club, the first thing he mentioned was Rush Limbaugh's letter!

After the Blue Room tea, the present and future first families gathered in the Grand Foyer waiting for the signal to board the motorcade on the North Drive for the procession to the Capitol, where the swearing-in ceremony took place. I found myself standing right next to the President-elect, so I struck up a conversation.

Chris: "One of my all-time heroes is from Arkansas."

President-elect: "Who's that?"

Chris: "Brooks Robinson (Hall of Fame Baltimore Orioles third baseman)."

President-elect: "Oh ya. He helped George Bush during the campaign."

Chris: "I didn't know that."

President-elect (looking at me strangely): "How did *I* know that?"

Chris: "No sir, I didn't know that he had helped President Bush."

The president-elect continued to give me an odd look. Suddenly, everyone was heading to the North Portico. I was thinking, "Awe man, the new president now thinks I'm some sort of GOP operative, questioning him like that. I was just trying to make conversation! I'd only thought, 'How cool that my childhood hero Brooksie, old number five, the greatest third-baseman of all time, just happened to be from Arkansas.' I had no clue Brooks had helped George Bush. Geesh, another great start, Emery!"

***

By 10:55 a.m., all parties had boarded their respective limousines and, as they were pulling out, President Bush looked at the ushers standing in the North Portico doorway. I gave him a thumbs up, and he returned the gesture as they drove off. That was it! Off to my duty station, the third floor in the Executive Residence.

The next hours would be mass mayhem.

The first adjustment for the Residence staff was dealing with the large volume of "handlers" the Clintons had invited to help with the move. The White House staff had been doing this routine quite well for the past 200 years. But here were people in the private residence no one had any idea about. The Secret Service couldn't keep up with clearing all these folks. We had several maids from the Arkansas Governor's Mansion that needed to be escorted at all times while inside the White House because they failed security screening. None of these Arkansas helpers knew their way around the White House and were all over the place. We lost track of them—too many of them and not enough of us!

For example, Chelsea had a live-in nanny, plus the nanny's mother would help with two or three other "helpers" tagging along. One woman was charging around the second floor with an earpiece and walkie-talkie, continually barking orders to what must have been a remote army.

The phones in the Ushers Office rang nonstop for three straight days. Chief Usher Gary Walters along with assistant ushers Skip, Dennis, and I, plus Nancy, our administrative assistant, Budget Administrator Worthington, and the staff from the Curator's Office were all working in a futile attempt to manage the chaos.

That evening, the new president set off a frantic search for his tuxedo, declaring he was already late for the first of the inaugural balls. We scrambled every direction to figure out where the Arkansas "helpers" may have placed it. The search ended successfully when the housekeeper located the tux in a random third-floor closet.

***

It happened that Inauguration Day, January 20th, fell on my day off. This, of course, didn't matter because all members of the Residence staff were required to be on duty. I worked from 5:30 a.m. to 12:30 a.m. and slept in the ushers' suite in the basement of the White House. Skip was on duty when the Clintons got in at 2:30 in the morning. It seemed they'd attended nearly every one of the inaugural balls.

Thursday, January 21, 1993 – *An Early Encounter*

I was in the office by 5:45 a.m. At precisely 7 a.m., a pair of young Clinton staffers brought the president's schedule and told me he was expecting it, that he had to have it right away. Knowing that no one upstairs was awake yet, I assured the staffers it would be taken care of. The two looked at each other, reluctant to leave this responsibility to me. Had I not been there, I believe they would have attempted to deliver it upstairs themselves.

I took the schedule, told the staffers I would call them in their office should anything be needed, then got on the elevator and headed to the second floor. I got off on two; it was quiet as the elevator doors closed behind me. I carefully opened the door to the private residence as quietly as possible. I looked into the Cross Hall where it was still dark. I could barely make out my target 15 steps away—the table at the entrance to the West Sitting Hall. For the past 75 years, the custom was for ushers to leave items for the president and first lady on that table. I walked there almost on my tiptoes to not make a sound.

While I had been doing this for years, I never felt at ease entering the private residence. This was the first family's sanctuary, their personal area. I always felt like I was I intruding. I was relieved as I placed the folder on the table, mission accomplished. But as I turned to leave, someone startled me. I was confused, might this be one of the Arkansas helpers that somehow stowed away? To my shock, as the person approaching got closer, I could finally recognize—it was Mrs. Clinton!

She was wearing a heavy red robe, but what threw me off were her thick glasses and long hair. She looked, well, like one would expect of someone who's been out till the wee hours of the morning. In a half whisper, I said, "Good morning."

She glared at me, probably wondering what the heck I was doing there. I quickly explained how I was delivering the president's schedule. She took the folder from the table and said, "I'll take care of this." I said something like "have a great day" and made a hasty exit. On the way back to the Ushers Office, I thought, "Man, I'm not making a good impression with this family thus far."

***

Later that afternoon, I had to call Mrs. Bush in Houston to tell her she'd accidentally written the wrong amount on a check she had left with me. It was for the vendor who delivered the HP Laser III printer I'd ordered for her. I called via the White House admin operator and President Bush answered. "Hey, Chris, Ranger (the president's dog) and I are coming over for a jog!" He sounded great.

"How are things going, Chris?"

"A bit chaotic, but we're managing, sir."

***

Plans were underway for the first major social event, the annual White House Governor's Dinner. It was scheduled to occur during the Super Bowl, the biggest professional football game of the year. A tremendous amount of indecision regarding the dinner menu prevailed, and the new social secretary was struggling to get organized. Add to that was the mounting, unjust scrutiny of White House Executive Chef Pierre Chambrin.

Pierre was the fourth executive chef I'd managed during my eight years at the White House. When I arrived in January 1986, Swiss-born Henry Haller was in his 20th year as executive chef—the best person ever to have served as chef. An incredible talent with a positive, pleasant temperament, everyone loved Chef Haller. He retired in 1987, to be replaced by Jon Hill. Chef Hill lasted five months and was replaced by German Sous Chef Hans Raffert. After Raffert retired in 1992, we hired Pierre Chambrin, who was French. An excellent chef, Pierre had a great attitude. Unfortunately, a group of prominent American chefs sent a letter to the White House urging the appointment of an American chef. Just over a year later, the Clintons fired Pierre and replaced him with an American, Chef Walter Scheib.

***

Most members of the Clinton staff quickly realized we, the ushers, were the most cohesive and knowledgeable group in the White

House. As such, we fielded a high volume of phone calls and visits from various admin staffers regarding the craziest variety of things, such as event setup, questions on history, specifics on the fine arts collections, furnishings, and all kinds of White House trivia.

***

That day, I worked nearly 15 hours. The next day, Friday, I worked another 15 hours. Long days. Yet as the ushers were soon to learn, this would become the norm in the Clinton White House.

Saturday, January 30, 1993 – *White House First Impressions*

At 8:10 a.m., President and Mrs. Clinton departed for Camp David. This gave the staff a much-needed break, although several relatives and other guests remained in the Residence and expected meals, vehicles, movies, and more.

After only 10 days, here were my early impressions: Mrs. Clinton is very sharp and not warm by any means. The president has great energy; he's warm and engaging, although he can be somewhat distant at times. He has a fun personality. Early in the morning, he appears to be out of it and yet he only drinks decaf coffee. If ever anyone needed caffeine, it would be President Clinton.

Early observations about the first group of Clinton houseguests: The Clintons have many young, energetic friends who are a lot of fun, including Harry and Linda Bloodworth Thomason, and John and Patricia Garamendi. John would later serve as President Clinton's Deputy Secretary of Interior.

The Rodhams, Mrs. Clinton's parents, were quiet but warm and friendly to me. Tony and Hugh Rodham, Mrs. Clinton's brothers, at first seemed like 1940-era movie actors with their long trench coats and fedora hats.

Mrs. Virginia Kelly, the president's mother, was immediately my favorite. What a card! Warm, genuine, and a lot of fun. Her husband Richard was very agreeable to be around. Roger Clinton, the president's younger brother, liked to have fun. I first met him when I took White House physician Dr. Mohr up to Roger's room after a

151

worried guest had called for a doctor. I knocked a few times on the door to Room 326 then opened it to see Roger asleep in bed.

"Roger, Roger. ROGER, DR. MOHR IS HERE TO SEE YOU!" He stirred only a little. I left thinking that maybe he'd done too much celebrating.

Chelsea's nanny was 20-year-old Ellen Dickey—pretty, young, very sweet. She became a permanent resident of the White House during the Clinton years, living on the third floor. Ellen's mother, Robyn Dickey, a beautiful, warm woman, became a regular guest at the White House.

With so many houseguests the first days of the Clinton White House, the people blurred in my mind. But certain things stood out. Mrs. Clinton's parents and brothers quickly assumed the White House was their all-inclusive resort with free military-driven cars at their disposal. Before they knew better, Mrs. Clinton's brothers would use official White House cars to go shopping, run errands, and even pick up Congresswoman Barbara Boxer's daughter, Nicole.

The brothers and their guests would watch 16 mm movies in the Family Theater. These required a projectionist and they watched a large volume of these, so our staff was getting worn out. They all enjoyed the swimming pool, bowling alley, and tennis court plus meals prepared on demand by the world's finest chefs. The extended family also availed themselves to the medical facilities, doctor's and dentist.

***

President Clinton had a habit of jogging during early-morning rush hour in D.C., totally disrupting traffic. One morning, he went jogging with Nebraska Senator Bob Kerrey. They walked out the South Portico, jogged right past the waiting motorcade, and then ran out the Southeast Gate. Members of the press rushed to the ready and took off in hot pursuit!

***

Meanwhile, Mrs. Bush called me regarding her printer. During our conversation, she asked me how it was going. I said it was an adjustment to walk through the West Wing and see so many dressed-down men with earrings and Mohawk haircuts. Her response: "Chris, you're just getting old!"

Sunday, January 31, 1993 – *Super Bowl Sunday*

The day's big event was the Governors Dinner at the same time as the Super Bowl between the Dallas Cowboys and the Buffalo Bills. The plan called for Texas Governor Ann Richards and New York Governor Mario Cuomo to arrive at the White House earlier than the other governors to have a press photo op with President Clinton. The president's staff arranged for the photo op to take place in the third-floor Solarium.

Mrs. Clinton had travelled from Camp David to Philadelphia for the day, arriving back at the White House at 4:45 p.m. At 5 p.m., the admin operator called the Ushers Office to say the first lady was on the line. I had this conversation with her:

Mrs. Clinton: "Hi, Chris. I don't want any press in the private quarters."

Chris: "Great."

Mrs. Clinton: "Is there some place else they can do the photo op?"

Chris: "Yes, we've got plenty of rooms, Mrs. Clinton. Gary just walked in; let me ask him what he'd suggest. (I quickly conferred with Gary.) Mrs. Clinton, Gary suggested the Family Theater. We have that giant screen TV, and we can get it all set up."

Mrs. Clinton: "Good. Let's move it."

Chris: "Yes; we'll take care of it."

***

By 5:25 p.m., President Clinton had returned from Camp David. As he walked into the White House, Nancy Hernreich, director of Oval Office operations, with a half-dozen young staffers greeted the president. Hernreich explained to the president that Mrs. Clinton had changed the photo op with Governors Richards and Cuomo from the private residence to the Family Theater in the East Wing. He angrily walked toward the elevator and said for all to hear, "What? I can't believe that! That won't work!" He got in the elevator and with a raised voice said to the doorman, "Take me to the second floor! I'm going to take care of this."

The Clinton staffers seemed convinced their man, the president of the United States, would quickly remedy this situation and move the photo op back to the Solarium. I knew better. The brief exchange between the president and his wife indicated without doubt who was in charge. Fifteen minutes later, the president came downstairs and headed to the Oval Office with no mention of the photo op. We started readying the East Wing Family Theater.

Texas Governor Ann Richards arrived at 6:11 p.m., just minutes before the Super Bowl kickoff. As I greeted her at the South Portico, she looked at me and, with her down-home Texas charm, said, "Are all you new people finding things around here?" I mumbled that I wasn't new, but I was helping those who were. New York Governor Cuomo arrived 10 minutes later, his greeting a bit more distinguished as he shook my hand and we exchanged pleasantries.

***

The dinner that night made modern White House history for lateness, with the actual meal not served until 9:15 p.m. Throughout the dinner, I provided written Super Bowl score updates for the butlers to give to the president and vice president.

By the time the Super Bowl ended, the Dallas Cowboys had slaughtered the poor Buffalo Bills 52–17. President Clinton and Governor Richards left the State Dining Room and walked into the Ushers Office to phone the victorious Cowboys. Assistant Usher, Dennis Freemeyer was dealing with photographers and the White House TV people who quickly followed the president and governor. I was able to slip past the entourage and made a speedy escape, leaving poor Dennis trapped at his desk. This gave me a great opportunity to give him a hard time. I dashed down the back stairs to Secret Service post F1 on the ground-floor hallway, picked up the phone, and used an outside line to call the Ushers Office. I knew Dennis would answer immediately to avoid a ringing phone as he attempted to keep things quiet while the president and governor made their congratulatory phone call to the Cowboys. In a hushed voice, Dennis answered, "Ushers Office."

With the thickest Arkansas drawl I could come up with, I said, "Hi, I'm intaarested in aaaah taawer of tha What Hauze."

Trying to be cool, Dennis acted as if he hadn't heard me and again said, "Hello."

I repeated my opening line and added, "Ah git fourteen of ma bes frienz heeeer, weeze alls from Arkansaaaw, en they tuld me to call the Ushas office for a taawer. Kin ya help me?"

Dennis, whispering, said, "Bad timing" and hung up the phone.

I burst out laughing and raced up the steps to watch from the hallway outside the Ushers Office. Dennis appeared flustered while trying hard to look under control. I was laughing so hard, I had to lean against the wall to hold myself up!

***

As it turned out, the media chose not to report the president's and governor's call to the Cowboys. This shocked the young Clinton staffers; they couldn't believe the press wouldn't cover such an historic event. I thought, "Welcome to the White House."

Early Mornings – Late Nights

Friday, February 5, 1993 – *A Giant Arkansas Pasture*

Crazy day: six events, including a working luncheon with Canadian Prime Minister Brian Mulroney. After the lunch, I couldn't believe where the Mulroney departure-statement lecterns were positioned—a long way down on the South Lawn. The president and prime minister must have walked 60 yards to get to their microphones, making it look like a giant Arkansas pasture behind them. Plus the two lecterns were so far apart, I thought a duel might follow! Why? It was later explained that the president's communications team wanted more of the White House in view. Unfortunately, on TV, the expansive lawn by itself filled up the shot! Well, they'll learn.

Saturday, February 6, 1993 – *One Morning's Duties*

A few minutes before 9 a.m., President Clinton went to the Oval Office to deliver his first weekly radio address. When he came back, I escorted him upstairs so he could change his clothes to play golf. Ten minutes later, he came down carrying a hand full of stogies. One appeared already chewed on. He told me how the weather seemed to go bad when he played golf. One time in Little Rock, it had rained for six hours while he played. I told him if he found the day's wind and snow were too much, he'd at least have something to blame his score on.

At 9:55, the president departed the White House for the Trent Jones Golf Course in Warrington, Virginia. Accompanying the president were Vernon Jordan, a leading figure in the Civil Rights Movement and close advisor to the president, Associate Attorney General Webb Hubbell, and business entrepreneur Dennis Bakke.

***

Later in the morning, Mrs. Clinton called and asked which gate James Carville should come to for his meeting with her. I said, "Any gate," and asked for his information for admittance. She needed to call me back with his DOB and SSN as well as his phone number. I called him with directions to B-11, the South East gate. He arrived at 10:52 a.m.

An extremely funny and exceptionally bright individual, James Carville was instrumental in President Clinton's successful campaign and became an unofficial advisor to the president and first lady. I took him up to the West Sitting Hall, where he waited for Mrs. Clinton who was on a phone call. I knocked and told her Mr. Carville had arrived. Ramsey, the butler, got him a cup of coffee. Then I escorted him to the Lincoln Bedroom and gave him a brief tour. He was nervous about not being there when Mrs. Clinton got off the phone. As we headed back to the West Sitting Hall, Mrs. Clinton met us halfway.

Sunday, February 7, 1993 – *More Observations and Opinions*

On a cold, gray morning, I was seated in the Ushers Office at 8:08 a.m. All was quiet. With the remnants of the inaugural reviewing stand still visible from my window, it seemed like it was taking forever to remove all that stuff! I saw the Secret Service agents wearing running gear, but with the cold, I bet the president wouldn't go running and probably would go to church. Which is exactly what happened, and the agents looked great in church with their running gear!

***

The previous Thursday, Chief Usher Gary Walters was asked by the president's Chief of Staff's Office to reduce the Executive Residence staff from 97 to 88. Gary reduced the number to 89 but knew that any more cuts would be difficult, so they agreed to 89 for the time being. A review of the Residence staff was due; it hadn't been done for many years.

***

Those of us in the Ushers Office were constantly challenged with our bizarre schedules. Day shift was 5:30 a.m. to 3 p.m., evening shift was 3 p.m. until well after midnight, and on weekends, we often didn't leave for home until 2 or 3 a.m. With a new first family in the White House, we were struggling to adjust to the disorganization and constant last-minute changes as well as the brutal hours.

From my observations, the beginning of the Clinton White House was plagued with ineptitude, inexperience, and chronic disorganization beyond expectation. I kept saying things could only improve. Many Clinton staffers were young campaign workers fresh out of college, with low pay and virtually no experience. The new president was paying a steep price for that! But having young staffers around kept things fun. Their energy, wit, and personalities did keep us laughing!

The most experienced advisors to the president were James Carville, Paul Begala, and George Stephanopoulos—all very good men and the real brains behind the Clinton election victory. I also regarded Chief of Staff Mac McLarty as a decent, humble man with a kind disposition.

President Clinton had great ambition and energy. His list of goals grew exponentially with his initial priority being his economic plan. I learned he was enamored with JFK, whom he'd met at a Rose Garden ceremony in July 1963 when Bill Clinton was only 16 years old—a moment that helped shape his life. I regarded Mrs. Clinton as smart with great ambition and energy. The two of them made quite a dynamic first couple.

Friday, March 26, 1993 – *Barbra Streisand: The Legend, The Beautiful*

Earlier in the week, singer Judy Collins had been a houseguest; then we welcomed actress Barbra Streisand for a stay at the White House. I greeted Ms. Streisand as she arrived, but before I could show her to the Queen's Room, a young staffer whisked her over to the West Wing.

We also hosted what West Wing staff called VIPs—the Medavoys from Hollywood. Young and attractive, Patricia Medavoy reminded me of Melanie Griffith. Her husband Mike Medavoy, a successful Hollywood producer, was friendly. I quickly put them at ease with a tour and my stories about White House history.

***

Shortly after 7 p.m., guests arrived in the Old Family dining Room on the State Floor for a dinner the president was hosting for 19 senators. Afterward, everyone was invited for the 10 p.m. University of North Carolina versus Arkansas, Sweet-16 tournament game to be viewed in the East Wing Family Theater. As the dinner guests were beginning to make their way to the East Wing, I escorted President Clinton upstairs to retrieve his houseguests. Barbra Streisand wasn't quite ready. Not wanting to miss the tip-off, especially with his home state University of Arkansas in the big game, he asked me to bring Barbra to the Theater once she was ready. I waited until she came out of the Queen's Room. We chatted; she was very sweet. I asked her about the last time she'd come to the White House. "Never," she replied, stating she didn't agree with the policies of the Reagan or Bush administrations. She conveyed her opinion with no animosity, just as a matter of fact.

The Arkansas team played well, but North Carolina prevailed. Everyone really had a good time. At midnight, after most of the guests departed, the president hosted Barbra Streisand, the Medavoys, and three other staffers on a tour, which began by walking the South Grounds. Meanwhile, I waited in the Diplomatic Reception Room, taking the opportunity to rest my feet. Ten minutes later, they came back and I tagged along on the tour, helping out here and there. President Clinton knew White House history remarkably well.

When we got to the State Floor, I told the group that 10 presidents had played the Steinway grand piano, and that he could be number 11. I winked at Barbra Streisand. The president sat down and played Gershwin's "Summertime." He played like a young student would, but hey, he played. Chalk up number 11!

***

While we were touring the State Floor, the military signal operator called to say the president's daughter Chelsea was on the line for her father. Chelsea and Mrs. Clinton were in Little Rock to visit Hugh Rodham Sr., Mrs. Clinton's ailing father. I glanced at my watch—12:30 a.m. I told the president of the call and he asked me to take over the tour, which I gladly did. While we were on the Truman Balcony, the president rejoined us, looking sullen. When I asked about Chelsea, he gave me a nod and said, "She's okay." Clearly, he didn't want to discuss it. We all then went on the roof, and I took our guests on the catwalk, then to the rooftop greenhouse. Everyone had a blast.

Saturday, March 27, 1993 – *A Restless Evening*

At 5:05 p.m., I took Marine Orchestra Conductor Colonel Bourgeois upstairs to see President Clinton, who was playing the Coasters' "Yakety Yak" on the saxophone—*and* doing a great job of it! He planned to play the song at the Annual Gridiron Dinner that evening.

At 7:13 p.m., the president and all houseguests left for the Gridiron Dinner at the Capitol Hilton. Everyone got back at 12:30 a.m. and I ushered them up on the elevator. The president was apologizing to the guests for the dinner taking so long, but no one seemed to mind. As they got off the elevator, he pointed to me and said, "Next time, he goes in my place" Everyone laughed. I guessed he was referring to the abuse he received (albeit good natured) at the Gridiron Dinner.

***

At 12:53 a.m., I started my "search and destroy mission" on the second floor (meaning killing all the lights). I went up and gave a listen but didn't hear anything. I tiptoed into the Dining Room and held my breath. No sound, so I started turning off the lights.

I then walked through the salon and through Chelsea's guestroom, peering around to see if the president was in his temporary study in the Yellow Oval Room. Nope, great! I walked to the Cross Hall, looked west then east. All was quiet. Perfect! I was almost free to leave for home.

Next, I killed the East Sitting Hall lights and then noticed open doors to the Queen's and Lincoln Bedrooms. I didn't look in. Instead, I did an about face and headed toward the West Sitting Hall, when suddenly the president came out of the door near the elevator. He was still wearing his white tie and tails from the Gridiron Dinner. I thought about escaping down the Grand Staircase, but that would set off the alarm, so I continued walking toward him.

Even though the president saw me, he didn't react. He walked into the kitchen, so I followed him in and said, "Mr. President, I sure enjoyed hearing your history on the presidents during last night's tour."

"I hope I got most of it right."

"Absolutely."

As he opened the small fridge in the Pantry, he went on to say he'd studied presidential history. He held a couple of wine glasses and wondered if there was any red wine. Then he pulled a bottle of Chardonnay and said, "This looks like white." I agreed with him and thought, "Look, bud, I know nothing of wines, but there aren't too many red Chardonnays." I checked another fridge in the kitchen as he followed. "No red wine, sir," I reported.

"Don't worry about it."

"Sir, you have your last two predecessors beat on your knowledge of the history of the White House."

He told me about the large number of books he'd read on the presidents. His latest was titled *FDR*. I asked if he'd read *Truman* by David McCullough.

"Yes, and he (McCullough) is a friend of mine."

I mentioned a two-volume set by Dr. Seale about the White House as we walked. All the time, he held the two wine glasses, a bottle of wine, and a corkscrew.

Then he went over to the table near the door near the elevator and started going through some paperwork. He dropped a red folder and a few papers spilled out, so I picked them up and said, "Well, sir, I hope things turn for the best in Little Rock." I knew the president was due to leave at nine the next morning to join Mrs. Clinton and Chelsea to be by his dying father-in-law's side.

The president stopped shuffling his papers, looked up, and said, "Thanks, guy." I said goodnight and headed back to my office.

At 2 a.m., President Clinton called and asked if I could take Tylenol up to Mr. Medavoy. I thought, "If the guy didn't drink so much wine, maybe he wouldn't have a headache." I took him a bottle and finally left at 2:30 a.m. So much for a short night.

Thursday, April 1, 1993 – *Fools Follies*
For some reason, I really got into the April Fools act:
1) I emailed the entire staff using my boss's name, Gary Walters, that there would be a 1:30 meeting. Bring a pad and paper and BE PROMPT. Then I left at 1 p.m. for a dental appointment. Later, I found out Gary wasn't too amused.
2) I had a friend from outside call the Ushers Office and pretend to be Mrs. Clinton's diarist, regular White House guest, Diane Blair. The caller told John, the doorman, about a leak in the Solarium. John called the engineers saying it was urgent, and two of them practically flew upstairs. Meanwhile, Dennis, the duty usher, worried about the leak, called the plumbers, and told them to go clean out the gutters—in the middle of a rainstorm!
3) President Clinton was in Portland and not due back to the White House until April 5th. I called into the Ushers Office on the military signal line and imitated the signal operator and announced that the president had arrived at Andrews Air Force Base. This threw everyone into motion to prepare for the president's White House arrival—until the Secret Service confirmed President Clinton was *not* on his way home.

Not sure why I went so overboard, but it was a lot of fun and, fortunately for me, almost everyone took it good naturedly!

Thursday, April 21, 1993 – *Poor Scheduling*
What a day. Incredible! At 3:30 p.m., we had 12 heads of state on the State Floor for teas with President Clinton. This was the most heads of state at the White House at one time since 17 came for John

F. Kennedy's funeral. The teas were immediately followed by 1,000 guests in a huge tent erected on the South Grounds commemorating the Jewish Holocaust.

During the teas, the president came into the Ushers Office twice for phone calls with Senate Majority Leader George Mitchell. They were working to rescue the Jobs Bill, which ended up failing to pass in the Senate. At one point, I held two gin and tonics (one for Gary Walters; the other for me) and looked up to see President Clinton coming. I quickly put the drinks down and covered them with a napkin.

Due to the poor scheduling of these events and the length of time the teas with the heads of state lasted, the president ended up arriving two hours and 22 minutes late to the Holocaust event! Hundreds of angry guests had already departed. After the tent event, President and Mrs. Clinton walked over to Blair House, coming back via motorcade due to the heavy rains.

The President and Mrs. Clinton came into the Ushers Office to find an impromptu gathering. Gary, the first lady's assistant, a Social Office staffer, the doorman, and I were all there feeling a bit slap-happy after another long day. President and Mrs. Clinton joked with us, and we all had several good laughs.

Wednesday, May 12, 1993 – *Here She Is, Miss America*
The beautiful Phyllis George, Miss America 1971, was a White House guest for a few days. One evening she was about to depart for a dinner honoring Queen Noor, she called me 10 minutes before leaving, concerned and scared because we were experiencing a severe thunderstorm. I told her it was a typical Washington storm. As we were talking there was a tremendous clap of thunder and a large elm tree near the tennis court crashed down onto the south driveway!

A few minutes later John, the doorman, and I went up in the elevator to await Ms. George. Moments later she entered the elevator wearing a low-cut sexy black dress. She was absolutely breathtaking. As we rode down in the elevator, she was looking in the elevator mirrors and asked John if he thought her dress was too low cut. John's face became deep red! She then laughed as she realized he wouldn't give an objective answer! As we escorted her to the South Portico, John and I fought over who would hold the umbrella for her as she got into her car.

Phyllis George returned a few minutes before midnight. I escorted her to the Solarium, then I called houseguest and interior designer Kaki Hockersmith, saying, "Wake up and come up to the Solarium!"

Kaki came up a few minutes later. I got them wine and told them White House ghost stories. I could have stayed longer, but I got word the president was on his way back. So, I led Phyllis and Kaki to the Truman Balcony to watch the Marine One land. As soon as the chopper came into view, I said a quick goodbye and rushed down to greet the president.

As President Clinton and I walked into the Diplomatic Reception Room, I told him that Phyllis George and Kaki were on the Truman Balcony. He looked tired, but I knew once he would see Phyllis in that dress, he'd be fine. I was right.

Saturday, May 15, 1993 – *Looking for Sympathy?*

I went to the second floor to wait for President Clinton who was running 30 minutes late. He was scheduled to go to Andrews Air Force Base to play golf. As he got on the elevator, he looked at me and said, "The schedule was messed up. I didn't know I was supposed to leave at seven forty-five." It was as if he were looking for sympathy from me. I stared blankly at him and thought, "You weren't; you were supposed to leave at seven thirty!" He then said something about being up late. I mentioned we had served coffee to his waiting golf guests who were fine. He seemed a little bewildered, and I felt sorry for him.

As we got off the elevator, he went directly to a Secret Service agent and explained how he misinterpreted his schedule. We got to the Diplomatic Reception Room and he greeted his guests, apologizing again for being late. As we got closer to the South Portico door, the president looked out and, surprised, asked, "We're taking the chopper?" The agent fumbled with an answer, saying due to time restrictions they needed to fly. President Clinton didn't look pleased. I piped in and said, "With the Andrews Air Force Base Air Show going on, traffic is a mess out there." The president looked relieved by my answer as it justified the use of the chopper.

***

I watched as President Clinton put on an attractive purple golf jacket and then, holding his cup of coffee, worked the crowd of 15 staffers and guests as he headed toward the chopper. Then he turned to his golf buddies and motioned for them to follow. I thought, "Unbelievable. I feel sorry for this guy because no one on staff is getting him straightened out. This president needs a take-charge individual with solid experience to get the Oval Office organized and provide direction to the painfully inexperienced staff."

Press Conference

Thursday, June 17, 1993 – *It's Prime Time*

I was working evening shift; the president was scheduled to hold his first prime-time press conference in the East Room at 8 p.m. A senior member of the Clinton staff asked Gary Walters if one of the ushers could handle the charts to be used during the conference. Since I was on duty, I'd be handling the task. I was asked to be in the East Wing Family Theater at 6 p.m. for the rehearsal.

As I arrived at the Theater, several staff members looked at me, probably wondering what the heck I was doing there. I sat toward the back and watched the disorganized scene. Paul Begala was at the podium rehearsing a speech for a roast for James Carville. I really liked Begala; not only was he brilliant, but he had a great sense of humor. White House Director of Communications and Deputy White House Chief of Staff Mark Gearan was there. I had met him the night before when he and his wife arrived for a private dinner. He seemed quite capable to me. I saw a geeky-looking fellow who had four large charts with graphs depicting how well the economy would do under the Clinton budget. A dozen or so strap-hanger young staffers were sitting around, all talking excitedly.

Finally, at 6:25 p.m., David Gergen arrived. A recent addition to the Clinton staff, Gergen was an imposing figure—tall, serious, someone who evoked authority. Gergan was what had been missing in the Clinton White House. He had the proven experience and perfect stature to be the "adult supervisor," which was so needed in the administration. As he stood in the entrance, everyone got focused and the chaos ceased for the moment. Chief of Staff McLarty and George Stephanopoulos arrived next. Then the president's appointment secretary, Andrew Friendly, appeared and said the president went upstairs to take a rest. I thought, "A REST!? Less than two hours before the press conference and he's taking a rest!?"

David Gergen was trying to assemble order of the 20 or so staffers in the Theater. He kept having to close the door as junior staffers ran in and out, and I could see he was getting perturbed.

Everyone stood in a semicircle around him as he asked for National Security Advisor Tony Lake's Somalia update. Finally, a little after 7 p.m., the president arrived. At that point Gergen bellowed, "If you don't have a need to be in here, leave now." Several young staffers hustled to the door.

Mark Gearan waved me over, and I stood next to the easel at the front of the room. President Clinton stood near me at the podium. Bright lights were being set up as the communications team was taping the rehearsal for its historic perspective. The geeky-looking guy holding the charts came over to me, obviously not pleased that a lowly usher would be handling his charts. He told me to place each one up on the easel and remove the old one, but I knew immediately that way was prone to error. So, I placed them in the proper order on the easel and removed them one at a time based on the president's remarks and action. This proved to work perfectly.

Next the staff took turns asking questions. Tony Lake started by asking about Somalia. The president gave him a blank stare and said, "I don't know. What's the answer?" Stephanopoulos then asked a question, then Dee Dee Myers, Leon Panetta, Mac McLarty, even Vice President Gore—all took turns firing questions at him. President Clinton did well adlibbing, but numerous times, he gave a blank stare to the questioner and asked, "What's the answer?"

Finally, at 7:45 p.m., David Gergen said "enough" and asked that all the nonessential persons leave the room to give the president a few minutes. I immediately headed to the door, but as I got there, I felt a hand on my shoulder. Gergen pointed for me to go back to where I was. I still don't know why he did that. Maybe he thought I would leak info to the press or for some reason decided I was indeed "essential"—HA!

Everyone left except for five or six top staff and a makeup lady who was working to cover an ugly fever blister under the president's nose. The president sat back in a large theater chair off to the side. Andrew Friendly was showing Media Advisor Mandy Grunwald and Press Secretary Dee Dee Myers three optional neckties for him. More people began discussing the ties. I stepped up and said

I thought the tie the president already had on was fine and everyone agreed.

Press Office Aide Ann Edwards came in and said we only had three minutes before the doors opened to the press. David Gergen and Mark Gearan came over to me looking quite concerned. Was I comfortable with my role in handling the charts? I smiled and said, "No problem." Ann Edwards then helped me carry them up to the East Room as the geeky-looking guy had long disappeared.

As I walked out of the Family Theater carrying the charts with Ann, Vice President Gore came up and said, "Make sure you put them up on the stage turned around so the press can't see them until we start." As I finally got up to the State Floor, another press aide, Steve Rabinowitz, "Rabi", told me to put the charts on stage a minute into the president's opening remarks and not before. I confirmed this with Mark Gearan and Ann Edwards. Everyone was so nervous. I stayed relatively calm, trying to understand what the big deal was.

As I walked up onto the dais, I looked down to see several junior members of the administration's staff sitting on the floor in front of the press. I leaned over and told them, "I'm going to place the charts upside down." As I stepped away, I could see the horror and panic in their eyes.

***

At one point, President Clinton reached inside his lectern for water. Oh crap! We forgot the water. Minutes (which seemed like hours) later, John, the doorman, appeared with a silver tray and glass of water. The president thanked him, then good naturedly joked that John had always wanted to be on TV, and he hoped his mother was watching.

Throughout the press conference, the president showed a lot of spirit and good-natured humor. Immediately after, he traded neckties with a reporter and gained a Mickey Mouse tie. Moments later, the president reentered the East Room to answer questions—wearing the new tie.

The press conference went well, including my part, and I couldn't believe how similar the press's questions were to those asked during rehearsal. Uncanny.

***

Shortly after the press conference, an impromptu meeting took place in the Ushers Office with President Clinton, David Gergen, George Stephanopoulos., Mac McLarty, Mandy Grunwald, Dee Dee Myers, and Mark Gearan. All were in high spirits as they recapped the event. The president noticed John the doorman nearby and said, "John, you're going to start getting fan mail. All the girls will write to you asking where you got your haircut." Everyone laughed. It was great to see an event like this come off so well.

President Clinton addressing the nation during his first prime-time press conference, with author Chris Emery handling the charts, June 17, 1993 (Official White House photo)

Tragic Death

Mid-July, 1993 – *A Cool Guy*

Late in the afternoon, I was at my desk in the Ushers Office when Deputy White House Counsel Vince Foster came up the back stairs and stepped into my office. He smiled, said hello, and asked if Gary Walters was still in.

"No, he's left for the day," I said.

"No problem. I'll catch up with him later." Vince turned and headed down the steps. A tall, tanned, good-looking man, he had an air of confidence—seemed to be a cool guy.

A longtime, close friend of President and Mrs. Clinton, Vince Foster had been handling a lot of personal legal matters for the Clintons. A former partner at the Rose Law Firm in Little Rock, Arkansas, he was instrumental in hiring Hillary Clinton to the firm as an associate in 1978.

Tuesday, July 20, 1993 – *All Hell Broke Loose*

With White House Chief Usher Gary Walters on vacation, I was acting chief for the week. After a long day at the White House, I had gotten home after 6 p.m. A short while later, I received a call from Dennis Freemeyer, the usher on duty, saying all hell was breaking loose. Vince Foster had been found dead in Fort Marcy Park, just outside of Washington. Chelsea's nanny Helen Dickey was in the Ushers Office sobbing hysterically. Dennis and John couldn't calm her down. She insisted on seeing President Clinton.

Dennis wanted to give me a heads-up, so I'd know about it when I came in the next morning. He sounded rushed.

The following is an excerpt from the ushers' log for July 20, 1993. (The ushers maintain a detailed log of all the movements of the first family. The log tracks all arrivals, departures, mealtimes, guests, etc.) This entry illustrates how busy July 20th was and the activities happening in and around the time of Mr. Foster's death:

Tuesday, July 20
7:30 Wake up call for the President
7:40 The President out for a jog
8:25 The President to the Oval Office
8:46 The President to the Second Floor
9:12 The President to the Oval Office
9:30 The President to the Rose Garden to announce FBI nominee Fhree
9:46 The President to the Oval Office
12:00 Lunch for Carolyn Huber and Janet Reinsch
12:43 The President and guests to Old Family Dining Room for
lunch (10 guests)
2:05 The President to Second Floor
2:10 The President to the Red Room
2:22 The President departs South Grounds for Capitol Hill
3:53 The President to the Oval Office
7:25 The President to the Second Floor
7:30 Dinner for the President
8:48 The President to the Library for the "Larry King Show" broadcast
10:00 The President to the Second Floor with Mr. McLarty and two staff
10:35 The President and staff down
10:40 The President out locally
12:10 The President, Mr. McLarty, Mr. Jordan, and Mr. Gergen to the
Second Floor
12:50 Marcia Scott and Amb. Cantor to the Second Floor
1:15 Robyn Dickey to the Second Floor
1:25 Mr. McLarty down
1:27 Mr. Jordan, Mr. Gergen and Ambassador Cantor down
2:00 Retired

Wednesday, July 21, 1993 – *Struggling Through It*

I arrived at the White house at 5:40 a.m. As the city of Washington awoke, the White House staff began to arrive. Clinton staffers were devastated by the news of Vince Foster's death. Everyone was in shock, understandably, and no one could believe it had happened. The number two man in the White House Counsel's office had been such a steady, long-time, key friend and confidant of the Clintons.

The president ate breakfast at 8 a.m. and then went to the Oval Office. I was attending to other matters, so the doorman ran the elevator and I didn't get a chance to see President Clinton until 11:28 a.m. That's when he returned from the Oval Office and I escorted him in the elevator to the private quarters on the second floor. I told him I was very sorry to hear about Mr. Foster and asked how the family was doing. The president, quite choked up, thanked me and said the family was struggling through it.

At 12:06 p.m., the president went over to Room 450 in the Executive Office Building where he and Chief of Staff Mac McLarty talked to the assembled staff about Vince Foster. I didn't attend, but evidently specific information was presented at this meeting because afterward, everyone was saying how depressed Vince Foster had been and what a tragedy that he took his own life. In a matter of minutes, the Clinton staff went from confusion and doubt to being on the same message, that Vince Foster had been troubled, under tremendous pressure, and thus that was the reason he he had taken his own life.

Scheduled for 12:30 p.m. that day was a business luncheon for CEOs in the Old Family Dining Room. All the guests had already arrived. On his way back from Room 450, the president stopped in the Rose Garden and spoke emotionally to the press about Vince Foster. At 12:55 p.m., I escorted the president, David Gergen, Mac McLarty, and others to the State Floor. They were all talking about the president's message recorded by CNN at the press conference. As President Clinton got off the elevator, I patted him on the back and said, "Good job, Mr. President." He turned and thanked me.

Friday, July 23, 1993 – *Funeral Day*
This was the day of Vince Foster's funeral in Little Rock. A lot of houseguests spent the previous nights at the White House, including those especially close to Foster—Carolyn Huber, Robyn Dickey, and Patsy Thomason. The West Wing asked the Ushers Office to order military vehicles with drivers to take people to Andrews Air Force Base for their flight to Little Rock. We needed a total of four vans for 16 people. I wondered about people from outside the White House using military vehicles and flying out of Andrews AFB, a military base. The White House military vehicles were for the express use of the president. Was this okay during exceptional circumstances? Fortunately, given the tragic circumstances, no objection was made for this situation.

President Clinton, Mrs. Clinton, and the entourage departed the White House at 8:15 a.m. Later in the daily press briefing, Dee

Dee Myers was deluged with questions concerning Vince Foster. Clearly, she wasn't prepared for the volume or type of questioning. Most of them asked about foul play and why this happened.

Wednesday, July 28, 1993 – *A Special Meeting Called*

At 8:20 p.m., Chief of Staff Mac McLarty and Deputy Chief of Staff Roy Neel went up to the private residence to meet with President and Mrs. Clinton for exactly two and a half hours. Then Neel called the Ushers Office about meeting with all the ushers at 8:30 a.m. the next morning. Neel said there would be something in the press concerning the Ushers Office related to Vince Foster's passing, so he wanted to tell us what was and wasn't about to happen.

Thursday, July 29, 1993 – *The Meaning about the Note*

When I arrived at the Ushers Office at 5:45 a.m., I quickly scanned the newspapers. Nothing out of the ordinary—there was a mention of finding a torn-up note in Vince Foster's briefcase. But what would that possibly have to do with the Ushers Office?

Our scheduled 8:30 a.m. meeting with Roy Neel didn't start until 10 a.m. When Mr. Neel appeared, we introduced ourselves then proceeded to the Map Room on the ground floor. We sat in a circle as Neel talked about Vince Foster and the note that had been found. He mentioned how Vince may have been under stress and perhaps not using clear judgment when he wrote it. No, it wasn't a suicide note but rather some random thoughts.

He went on to say what Foster wrote in no way reflected the Clinton Administration's view. It was *not* an official memo. The note mentioned an Ushers Office "plot" regarding the costs of the Clinton private quarters renovations and mentioned the name of Clinton decorator, Kaki Hockersmith. Neel cautioned the word "plot" would likely attract press attention. He again reiterated this in no way reflected the Administration's view of the Ushers Office, that the Ushers Office was doing a good job supporting the first family and even the president and first lady had mentioned it.

Neel said he wasn't sure the actual note would be released to the press; the decision would be made by the president and Mrs.

Foster. Neel then said they hoped this would not snowball into something as unfortunate as the Travel Office episode. I thought, "Wow, what a reach!" What an odd thing to correlate to this situation.

The reference to the Travel Office got all of our attention. The Travel Office controversy, better known as Travelgate, was a highly publicized event in May 1993, when the Clinton White House alleged wrong-doing and terminated seven career federal employees who managed the official travel for the Clinton Administration. Years later, all seven of the Travel Office employees were cleared of any wrong-doing. Travelgate brought on several investigations of President and Mrs. Clinton that continued long after that.

Gary Walters mentioned that, in his last meeting with Mr. Foster, they had discussed the renovations and a concern about their cost. Roy Neel realized this note could force the Clinton Administration to reveal the high expense of the private residence renovations—exceeding $300,000 and growing. The extreme costs were mostly due to poor project planning and excessive use of over-priced materials.

The meeting concluded with Gary thanking Mr. Neel for his time. Neel left the room and Gary's assistants, Skip, Dennis, and I couldn't move; we felt numb. We worked so hard to never be noticed or mentioned by the media, and we all realized everything was about to change.

Tuesday, August 10, 1993 – *Note Released to the Press*

The Clinton Administration released Vince Foster's torn-up note—actually, a text version, not a copy of the original handwritten note. One of the last lines in his "note" stated, *"The Ushers Office plotted to have excessive costs incurred, taking advantage of Kaki and HRC (Hillary Rodham Clinton)."* The remainder of the note was strange, with high praise for the Clintons and their loyal staff, and a pledge that there had been no wrongdoing—all seemingly rather self-serving for the Administration. After the transcript was released at 2 p.m., the Ushers Office became inundated with calls from the press.

Later, David Gergen stopped by the Ushers Office as he was leaving the East Room where Justice Ruth Bader Ginsburg's swearing-in had just occurred. He asked me how we were handling the high volume of calls. "No problem. We simply refer them all to the Press Office," I responded. Gergen said he believed that by releasing info quickly to the press, this would die down soon.

***

At 4:05 p.m., Mark Gearan led the afternoon press briefing, with the majority of the questions dealing with the Ushers Office. At one point, Mark stepped away from the podium and came back seconds later with a sheet detailing the costs of the second-floor private residence renovations. At the same time, I received a call from the admin operator with an urgent call for Mrs. Clinton, who was in the Yellow Oval Room doing a photo shoot. Jeff, the electrician, was helping with the lighting for the photo shoot and was near the first lady when she took the call. An angry Mrs. Clinton was heard saying she didn't want the renovation costs released to the press. She hadn't agreed to this action, and she was washing her hands of the entire episode.

The next day, the Clinton Administration announced that the White House Historical Association would be paying for the Clinton renovations. At that time, new presidents were allotted $50,000 to make renovations to the second-floor private residence and Oval Office. With the Clinton's total bill exceeding $350,000, the Historical Association had a lot to cover!

Dog Days of Summer

Sunday, August 29, 1993 – *Oval Office Awe*

The first family would be returning close to midnight from their Martha's Vineyard vacation. Clinton friend and interior decorator Kaki Hockersmith was upstairs; the first lady's mother and brother were staying on the third floor. The final touches to the now infamous private residence renovations were completed. Renovations were for the Lincoln Sitting Room, the Master Bedroom, and the Oval Office

Early in the morning, I went to check out the Oval Office. This would give me an opportunity to see the renovations, and with the first family and staff gone, I could take my time and fully look at the most famous and powerful office in the world.

I arrived to see Secret Service Uniformed Officer Larry Householder at post E6 at the door. The heavy curved door to the office was closed. I told Larry I had business to take care of, then I opened the door and unhooked the velvet stanchion to enter. I joked to Larry that I didn't want to be disturbed.

I entered the office and my first sight was the magnificent HMS Resolute desk, which had been a gift from Queen Victoria of Britain in 1880. It was the same desk under which President Kennedy's son John-John could be seen playing in photographs. I walked across the beautiful deep blue oval rug with its bright gold presidential seal in the middle. The floor-to-ceiling drapes perfectly matched the color of the gold seal on the rug and two out-of-place-looking red-striped sofas. I then opened the door to the back rooms, the main door where I'd entered slammed closed from a draft. Suddenly, I stood all alone in the Oval Office. Cool! I had been to the Oval Office many times, but often when the president was there or when I'd gone to retrieve something. I never had the luxury to take my time, look around, and enjoy the room.

As I walked through the office and adjoining suites, I saw photos of President and Mrs. Clinton in the hallway leading to the small dining room. I noticed several framed political button collections hanging and low bookshelves that featured books on the bottom shelves and photos on the upper ones. The Oval Office bathroom with "500" on its door sported framed political cartoons. On a corner shelf were lots of Allergy Bee Gone containers that President Clinton relied on to battle his allergies. The small study across and down the short hallway from "500" looked comfortable. It had paintings and tons of photos, including a framed check from Bob Dole for building the White House jogging track. The display sported a humorous inscription about cutting presidential fat.

When I exited the Oval Office five minutes later, Officer Householder asked the reason for my visit to fill out the official log. I quipped, "I was looking for the missing eighteen minutes from the Nixon tapes!"

***

Back in the Ushers Office, I received a call from an aide to the president informing me that Senior Aide David Gergen, Defense Secretary Les Aspin, and other senior administration officials would be playing tennis on the White House court later that afternoon. "Yes," I said. "I'll make sure the court is in good shape." The aide then asked, "Is there a fridge out at the court?"

"No longer. Gary Walters had the engineers move it up to the nanny's room."

"Then could we have a cooler out there filled with refreshments?"

"Yes, I'll take care of it."

***

Next, I called Mrs. Clinton's mother, Mrs. Rodham, about her meal plans for the day. Because she hadn't been feeling well, I thought she might want to have breakfast for lunch so I told her I would have the chef call her when he arrived. Mrs. Rodham was a sweet lady—not nearly as fun as the president's mother Virginia Kelley, but Mrs. Rodham was always gracious and kind.

***

Mrs. Rodham and Mrs. Clinton's brother Hugh were leaving for Pennsylvania for a few days. I went up to help with luggage; heck, I not only helped but I did it all, except for one of the maids carrying Mrs. Rodham's hanging clothes. Hugh's giant bag weighed close to half what he did! And Mrs. Rodham had a huge, heavy suitcase. With one heavy suitcase in each hand, I had a tough time steadying myself.

We all got on the elevator. Hugh was wearing shorts and a t-shirt which didn't quite cover his belly, he was eating a green apple.

Once on the ground floor, Hugh got off the elevator before me, but "his eminence" didn't even offer to help with the luggage. I struggled to get the bags to the South Portico. My back still isn't right. In retrospect, I couldn't help but laugh at myself. Here I was, age 36, wearing an expensive business suit and in the prime of my illustrious eight-year White House career. Yet I was carrying these damn bags filled with pyramid stones, all while this man was walking ahead of me like a king. Maybe I should have held his apple for him!

I kept thinking how various family members and guests would never *not* offer to help. This humbling experience served to bring me down to earth and realize my role is purely as a serf. It also caused me to ask, "What am I going to do when I grow up?" Working in the Ushers Office was an amazingly great experience; however, I realized I would never glean a great sense of accomplishment. I would simply get old dealing with all the super egos.

***

I knew houseguest interior decorator Kaki Hockersmith was having a quiet dinner alone in the family kitchen, so I went up to see her. I could hear soft music playing from the first family's massive stereo system located between their bedroom and the TV room. The music was soothing and relaxing. I talked with Kaki in the kitchen for a few minutes, then said goodnight.

As I was walking out, a song was just ending on her CD, somehow I remembered that Kaki was not a fan of Elvis. I dashed over to the stereo and stuck in a CD of Elvis Live. I couldn't resist. After setting the volume to max, I ran out, laughing. As soon as I got back to the Ushers Office, the phone rang. Kaki was laughing, too, saying she couldn't believe I could find something so obnoxious. It was easy I thought, "President Clinton had a large collection of Elvis CDs in the White House."

Fall Events

Tuesday, September 14, 1993 – *My evening with Julia Roberts*
The Clintons enjoyed hosting many small to mid-sized private dinners. They'd occur in either the Blue Room on the State Floor, in the second-floor private residence, outdoors on the terrace outside the Red, Blue, and Green rooms, or occasionally on the Truman Balcony.

At 7 p.m., 20 guests arrived at the Diplomatic Reception Room for cocktails. Among those coming late were Julia Roberts and her then-husband Lyle Lovett. President and Mrs. Clinton had just left the room with several guests to take them to the second floor when Julia and Lyle walked up to me and introduced themselves. I said hello and that my name was Chris, acting as if they were like anyone else, which I believe they appreciated. Julia was polite, beautiful, and a bit nervous as many are when they first enter the White House. I decided to put her at ease by sharing White House trivia, so I leaned close and asked, "Do you know what happened in this room?"

Julia looked at me and said, "No, what?"

"When the White House was built, this was the boiler room, and the first baby's birth in the White House happened to be right here in this room!"

With that, I had her full attention. "Do you know who the mother was?" She shook her head no.

"A slave."

I then asked if she had any idea who the father was. Before she could respond, I said, "Thomas Jefferson!"

Julia smiled and said, "Wow." Then she slipped her arm though mine and said, "I'm staying close to you all night!"

After escorting them up to the private residence, we entered the Lincoln Bedroom where I provided more history. By this point, other guests had gathered to listen. We went on to the Lincoln Sitting Room, then across the Hall to the Queen's Room. We continued to talk as I showed them around, being interrupted often by other guests who wanted to meet them. Each time someone would approach Julia and Lyle, I'd back away. As soon as the interrupters were done, they would seek me out to talk and learn more historical trivia.

Thursday, October 7, 1993 – *Mess in Somalia*

At 6:25 p.m., I was on the ground floor next to the elevator as President Clinton approached. Wearing a navy-blue suit and red tie with thin blue stripes, he looked tall, strong, and determined. However, I could see he was upset. He held my upper arm as he walked into the elevator. The president had just concluded an address to the nation about Somalia, stating his outrage with the way the Somali gangs had desecrated the bodies of American soldiers by dragging the dead U.S. servicemen through the streets. Here's how our discussion went:

President Clinton: "I sure hope I'm doing the right thing in Somalia; it's just so hard."

Chris: "It's tough, very frustrating. You came across well in your address."

President Clinton: "Thank you. I conferred with General Powell and Admiral Crowe. They agreed this was the thing to do— get our job done and then get out. But we can't just pull out; we have to complete the job. It sure made me mad to see them drag our soldiers through the street like that."

Once the elevator had reached the second floor, the two of us stood there awhile, the president was in no hurry to leave. I was amazed how candidly he talked that evening, as if he needed someone to share his feelings with.

Chris: "Seeing that just tears your heart out."

President Clinton: "I've never been so mad. The hostages in Iran made me mad but not like this. I could kill those people."

Chris: "So, you spoke to Admiral Crowe?" (William James Crowe, Jr., was the United States Navy admiral who served as chairman of the Joint Chiefs of Staff under Presidents Ronald Reagan and George H. W. Bush. He served as ambassador to the United Kingdom under President Bill Clinton.)

President Clinton: "Yes."

Chris: "How is he?"

President Clinton: "Fine."

Chris: "He was such a character."

President Clinton: "I'm in the habit of calling a lot of the former authorities to get their opinions."

Sunday, October 10, 1993 – *Let's Plant a Tree*

Working evenings, I got to the White House at 2:45 p.m. Groundskeeper Dale Haney told me he was waiting on Mrs. Clinton to do a tree planting on the South Grounds. I called Mrs. Clinton, who pleasantly expressed concern about dragging in a photographer on the weekend for a photo shoot. I told her we always had a photographer on duty, and that I'd find out who was available and call her back. Then I paged the duty photographer, Barbara Kinney, who said she'd be at the White House in 20 minutes. I conveyed that to Mrs. Clinton, who kept covering the phone receiver and asking the president what he wanted to do. Finally, she said, "When does Dale want to plant the tree?" Dale was standing next to me, so I asked him. "Well, today would be fine around four o'clock." Mrs. Clinton replied, "Okay, we'll be down at four o'clock." But then she called me back at 4:10 and told me they'd also be taking a bike ride—and could I find bicycles for them? I ran around the White House basement storage areas and discovered Bill Clinton's red bike had a flat tire. The engineers couldn't fix it quickly, so I brought out a super cool black mountain bike that had belonged to President Bush.

President, Mrs. Clinton, and Sox the cat came down at 4:20. The president wore a sports shirt and sports jacket, while Mrs. Clinton in her navy blue dress looked much dressier than her husband. The president carried Sox, who was attached to a very long leash. We all headed to the South Portico where the bikes were. When the president asked where the black one came from, I replied, "It belongs to the White House."

We walked along the South Drive to the area near the walkway to the Oval Office, where Dale was waiting with the ceremonial shovels. There, President and Mrs. Clinton took turns piling dirt on the tree. As we moved to the next target, the president held one end of the leash and Sox ran alongside us.

The second tree to be planted was near the tennis court where they again both threw a few shovels of dirt for the camera, then on to the final tree to the northeast of the South Fountain. Again, they took turns shoveling while Barbara snapped photos. I thought, "Wasn't one of these trees supposed to be planted by only Mrs. Clinton?"

Meanwhile, Sox and his 20-foot leash had become hung up inside a miniature Japanese maple tree. Before I could react, the president was crawling under the tree to free the cat! I felt helpless seeing the leader of the free world on his hands and knees rescuing a cat. Mrs. Clinton and I began to laugh at this scene. The president mockingly thanked us for our support, then they quickly went back inside so they could change clothes for their bike-riding excursion.

***

On their way out for the bike ride, the president asked me to set up the movie *Bronx Tale* and said they'd have dinner in the Theater when they got back. Then off they went to ride on the George Washington Parkway (hmm, I thought that was a freeway), returning an hour and a half later.

Mrs. Clinton waited as her husband went up to the second floor. While in the elevator, the president asked me to get a bottle of champagne for their dinner—the eve of their anniversary.

***

When I came down, I found Mrs. Clinton in the China Room. We talked about the various sets of china on display, and I told her how President Bush had used the Lincoln China for a luncheon with Prince Charles. Then I mentioned the Team 100 dinners, in which both Reagan-era and Johnson-era china were used. She asked me what Team 100 was, and I explained it consisted of individuals who had donated at least $100,000 to the GOP. I commented, "I can't believe someone would spend $100,000 for a political party."

She replied, "It would be like you giving a hundred dollars, Chris."

I thought, "Heck, I wouldn't give a hundred dollars to any political party!"

Thursday, October 14, 1993 – *Hostage Freed*

At 6:53 a.m., I took a call from George Stephanopoulos asking if the president was awake. "Yes, the president had a six-forty-five wake-up call."

"The American hostage in Somalia has been released. Would you please inform the president?"

"Yes, I'll take care of it." I went directly up to the second floor. As I walked into the center hallway in the dark, I was startled to see a person standing there—a houseguest waiting to go for a run with the president. I introduced myself, which also gave me a chance to see if he knew where the president was. I found the president in his dressing closet, just as he was grabbing his running shoes.

Chris: "Mr. President, George Stephanopoulos just called and said the American hostage in Somalia has been freed. George is available if you need to call him."

President Clinton: "Let's get him on the phone."

Chris: "I can call him from the phone out here in the center hall."

Carrying his running shoes and socks, President Clinton followed me and said good morning to his running guest and told him he'd be just a minute. I picked up the phone and told the admin operator to ring George Stephanopoulos for the president, who was now seated on the chair next to me pulling on his socks.

The admin operator got George on the line.

George S.: "Mr. President?"

Chris: "George, stand by." I handed the phone to the president and headed back to my office while George passed on the good news. Moments later, the president and his guests left the South Grounds for their run.

Friday, October 22, 1993 – *The Unending Math Problem*

At 7:15 a.m., I called President Clinton to remind him today's jogging guest was waiting in the Diplomatic Reception Room. He asked me to let him know he'd be down after he'd helped Chelsea with her math homework.

About 15 minutes later (10 minutes after Chelsea had left for school) I saw the elevator being called to the second floor, so I jumped in and greeted the president as he got on. He began telling me in detail about Chelsea's math problem—calculating the duration of a wave in a stadium based on a sample of 16. He explained it to me in a way that seemed that he hoped I had the answer.

We walked into the Diplomatic Reception Room where he met his guest. As the three of us headed toward the South Grounds, the president ignored his running guest. Turning to me, he said, "Well, anyway. About this math problem . . . " We stood at the South Portico discussing it for a few minutes. I'm thinking, "I'm not a math wizard, I'm a computer guy and that's why we have computers to solve math problems." Meanwhile, the motorcade was running, press people were watching us, guests were waiting, and Secret Service agents were giving me the evil eye. I felt privileged that, in that moment, the president only cared about talking to me even if it was about a math problem. Meanwhile, I knew the ongoing delay was wreaking havoc by affecting the security detail, traffic closures, press deadlines, and more.

A short while later, when he returned from his run, the first thing the president asked me was, "Did you come up with a solution?"

"No, sir. Are you sure this is a high-school-level problem?" He laughed.

Tuesday, October 26, 1993 – *Greatest Party in White House History*

We held a surprise Halloween party for Mrs. Clinton's birthday—the most fun I've had during the Clinton Administration and maybe even in my entire time at the White House! Ushers aren't allowed to have this kind of fun, are they?

One hundred fifty guests came, all in costume. The Executive Residence staff dressed in costume, too. I was Paul Revere; the butlers were a combination of musketeers and colonial gentlemen. David Gergen came as a tall Richard Nixon. Chief of Staff Mac McLarty was dressed as a football player, Vernon Jordan drew a lot of laughs dressed as basketball great Michael Jordan. All the planning and preparation, orchestrated by Mrs. Clinton's staff, was done in total secrecy. Mrs. Clinton had no clue.

That evening, Mrs. Clinton came back from Capitol Hill at 7 p.m. At that time, every light in the Residence was off except for spotlights illuminating a giant 17 by 22-foot pumpkin on the North Portico. Chelsea's nanny, Helen Dickey took Mrs. Clinton upstairs where she found the president dressed as James Madison. The first lady's staff worked with a firm that had authentic, high-quality colonial-era costumes and they had a Dolly Madison costume for Mrs. Clinton!

At 8 p.m., President, Mrs. Clinton, and Chelsea walked down the Grand Stairs. Mrs. Clinton had expected to see Halloween decorations and perhaps a few staff members. Instead, she was greeted by more than 20 staffers, who performed a little skit and song. It was still completely dark except for the spotlight on the singing staff. Meanwhile, the 150 invited guests who had gathered were in the dark hallway and began singing "Happy birthday." Mrs. Clinton was totally surprised.

***

The party went on past midnight. At one point, I was in the East Room enjoying the band playing Jerry Lee Lewis music when Barbara Kinney, the White House photographer, grabbed me to dance. And dance we did, before I knew we were dancing next to President and Mrs. Clinton.

I could see my co-workers in background, all were staring at me in shock, thinking, "What the heck is he doing!?" I just laughed and kept dancing. This broke the ice. Ten minutes later, all of the staff were dancing, we danced the night away.

At another point, while I was standing in the State Dining Room, the president grabbed me for a photo with Mrs. Clinton. By then, he had removed his James Madison wig. I told him he now looked like Thomas Jefferson. Then he asked for a photo with the butlers, so I helped round them up and Dennis Freemeyer and I took over tending bar, which was a riot. Before long, the president was on stage in the East Room playing his saxophone. It was a great time had by all!

Mrs. Clinton (Dolly Madison), President Clinton (James Madison), author Chris Emery (Paul Revere), October 28, 1993 (Official White House photo)

Saturday, November 27, 1993 – *Defacement of the Fine Arts Collection*

Working at the White house never got old; sometimes the routine became, well, routine, so I would think of ways to make things fun. On some weekends, the Clintons traveled to Camp David, which gave for the Residence staff a welcome break from our regular duties. The ushers would often double shift, thus allowing the third usher to have an actual weekend off. That meant Saturday shifts would be from 7 a.m. until about 7 p.m. Not too bad.

Late one Saturday when the Clintons were away and most staff members were gone, I found a ladder on the State Floor. I thought, "The electricians must have left it there." Then I moved it to the main hallway between the State Dining Room and the East Room, closer to my target, the bust of Marquis de Lafayette. This bust was at least 14 feet from the floor in a small alcove above a doorway. It appeared that Lafayette was looking down his nose at those entering the State Dining Room.

Bust of Lafayette above the door on the State Floor of the White House (Emery personal collection)

In my hand, I had a bright red-and-blue ski cap lost by a tourist earlier in the day. So up the ladder I went, step by step, until I was in easy reach of the bust. I pulled the cap down over Lafayette's head, then climbed down and moved the ladder back to where I found it. I then called the night electrician and asked him to put the ladder away.

A couple of days later during the public tours, a commotion occurred on the State Floor. It seemed the tourists were stopping to look up at Lafayette wearing a bright colorful ski cap. This disturbance backed up the progress of the tours, so the Secret Service responsible for conducting the tours, immediately alerted the Ushers Office. In turn, we alerted the White House curator. The curator who arrived on the scene wasn't amused at this horrific act of defacement. I stood off to the side near the Secret Service tour officers and, along with hundreds of tourists, watched as a large ladder was hastily put in position for an electrician to climb up and retrieve the hat. The curator stood at the bottom of the ladder looking up and directing the operation.

The mystery was never solved, even though I'd given a perfectly logical explanation: Perhaps a spirit from White Houses past was pulling a prank. The curator returned my suggestion with a cold stare.

A Clinton Christmas

Wednesday, December 1, 1993 – *Comes with the Job!*

At 7:30 p.m., the guests began to arrive in the East Room for the black-tie Democratic National Committee dinner. I thought, "Where the heck will all these Democrats find tuxedos!?"

While in the elevator as I escorted President and Mrs. Clinton to the event, Mrs. Clinton looked at my tuxedo shirt.

Hillary C: "Bill, would you wear a shirt like his, the kind with the pointed collar?"

POTUS: "Sure (the president looking at me and smiling), but I wouldn't look as good as he does. Chris looks *good* in that shirt."

I thanked him with a smile.

***

Later that night and into the early morning hours, I had a long talk with Clinton friend and interior decorator Kaki Hockersmith. I've always enjoyed talking to Kaki, who has a great sense of humor and has earned the confidence of the Clintons. She told me how she could see and understand the Ushers Office's frustration with the disorganization of the first lady's inexperienced staff. She had been present when Mrs. Clinton told her top aide one thing and then that aide conveyed something different to the Ushers Office. "How is it you haven't pulled out your hair?!" she asked me.

Thursday, December 2, 1993 – *Christmas Tree Allergies*

The Christmas season officially kicked off with the early morning delivery of 27 evergreen trees. In the evening, the president and first daughter Chelsea came to the State Floor after visiting the doctor's office. (Poor Chelsea was sick.) I walked with them as they looked at the beautiful trees. The president told me how badly they affect his allergies and that in the previous year the doctors wanted to operate on him for his allergies! I wondered how he'd ever make it through all those Christmas party receiving lines surrounded by those trees.

191

***

During one of the White House Christmas parties, John, the doorman, and I got a little carried away. John wrapped a kilo of the bright white confectioners' sugar powder that had collected in the Christmas cookie trays into a cellophane brick. This cocaine-looking package, the size of a brick, looked like something from the TV show *Miami Vice*. We tossed it around the office, then I slid it inside a random staffer's coat pocket. We were laughing hard and thinking about the possible consequences of such a prank.

Monday, December 20, 1993 – *Trouble Afoot*

Thank goodness we were getting close to the end of the Christmas season at the White House! Days were long and there were very few days off. My weekly totals thus far for December, were 59, 64, and 58 hours a week. That may not seem like much, but it sure *felt* like a lot! The hardest part was having to work on all my days off during the holiday season.

The previous night for the Arkansas and Friends party, the president and first lady hosted a receiving line from 6:30 until 8:10 p.m. in the Diplomatic Reception Room. Then they went into the Map Room for a 15-minute briefing by Director of the Office of Presidential Personnel Bruce Lindsey. There, they got word of breaking news: At 8pm, CNN would lead with a 10-minute story about Bill Clinton's infidelity while governor of Arkansas.

The story centered around two Arkansas state troopers who claimed to have provided then-Governor Clinton with women for sex. After Lindsey's meeting, the president and Mrs. Clinton went up to the second-floor private residence. On the elevator, he was shaking his head saying he can't believe people would believe such a story.

After this type of news, I naturally figured the Christmas party would wind down, so I told the butlers to close the bars at 9 p.m. Then to my surprise, at 8:50, the Clintons came down to the party and kept the event lively. So much for closing the bars; the party raged on until till close to 11.

***

It was amazing. After nearly a full year with the Clinton Administration, each day seemed more disorganized. We hadn't seen any improvement in organizing the events managed by the first lady's East Wing staff. Her staff needed the equivalent of a David Gergen, whose presence had an immediate and positive impact on the president's West Wing staff.

Wednesday, December 22, 1993 – *The Last of the Parties*
        Guests began arriving for the Executive Residence staff Christmas party at 5:20 p.m. President and Mrs. Clinton did their receiving-line routine from the Diplomatic Reception Room. Afterward, they went upstairs and then 45 minutes later, left the White House for a private party in northwest D.C. I was disappointed they didn't mix and mingle as they had for every other party. But with this being the last of the Christmas parties, I'm sure they felt ready for the break. I was happy to see that the president's parents and brother Roger stayed at the party to the very end.

Saturday, December 25, 1993 – *Merry Christmas to Those Working*
        At 8:36 a.m. Christmas morning—a gray day with snowfall possible—I was at my desk in the Ushers Office. As I looked out the window, Lafayette Park seemed peaceful, its only activity a large flock of seagulls.

***

        That morning, the Secret Service agents were complaining because the first family's schedule had changed yet again. For the past several days, all facets of the first family's schedule had been problematic, from the overall timing to the smaller details. The previous night, Mrs. Clinton's aide told the ushers to have dinner prepared for 20 guests. Well, it ended up being served to only eight people! This affected not only the chefs but the number of butlers and kitchen personnel who had expected to handle a dinner for 20 people.
        At 9 a.m., I received a call from Mrs. Clinton's aide to confirm that Christmas dinner for 18 would be at 3 p.m. in the Old Family Dining Room. At 9:17 a.m., the president came back from a

meeting in the Oval Office. In good spirits, he had an armload of wrapped presents with a chewed cigar lying on top. We wished each other Merry Christmas. When I got back to my office, the phone rang. Mrs. Clinton wanted to know which people were working in the Executive Residence that day, so I put together the following memo:

Merry Christmas!!!

Executive Residence Staff here today. Ho! ho! ho!

Butlers—
> Sam (Ricardo Sanvictores)
> Buddy Carter
> Jim Ramsey (in the afternoon)
> Jim Selmon (in the afternoon)

Kitchen Staff—
> John Moeller
> Sean Haddon
> Roland Mesnier
> Pierre Chambrin (arrives at 11 a.m.)

Housekeepers—
> Christine Limerick
> Carmen Martins
> Mary Arnold
> Silvia da Silva
> Willie Shuford

Electricians—
> Mark Robbins (until 3:30 p.m.)
> Richard Chapman (arrives at 3:30 p.m.)

Engineers—
> Matt McCloskey (7 a.m. – 3 p.m.)
> Brian Rock (7 a.m. – 3 p.m.)
> Ron Smith (2:30 p.m. – 11 p.m.)
> Jim Atkinson (2:30 p.m. – 11 p.m.)
> Clark Fries (11 p.m. – 7 a.m.)
> Phil Whiston (11 p.m. – 7 a.m.)

Plumber—
> Bob Gallahan

Florist—
    Nancy Clarke
Ushers Office—
    Chris Emery (6 a.m. – 3 p.m.)
    Dennis Freemeyer (arrives at 3 p.m.)
I delivered this list to the Clintons with a Christmas card—one of the White House Historical Association cards with a drawing of the Blue Room. On it, I drew in green a Christmas tree and inside I wrote:

Merry Christmas!!!
How's this for a White House card?
Mr. President, your energy, youth, vigor, and determination have been an inspiration to all. Congrats on your first year in the White House and here's to keeping Rush Limbaugh "hostage" for another 7 years! HA!
Merry Christmas, and thanks for everything.

Chris Emery – Ushers Office

***

Later that morning, I took the White House doctor to see the president's mother, Mrs. Kelley. Both the president and Mrs. Clinton were in the hallway and greeted me in a friendly, warm way. Then Mrs. Clinton gave me a box of cedar/cinnamon air fresheners to give to those on staff who were "stuck" (her term) working that day.

They told me about the two ladies who started the company to make cedar bags. President Clinton laughed, adding the company grew to having "400 hillbillies working up in the mountains." They thanked me for working that day, saying how hard it must be. When I asked how they liked last evening's service at the National Cathedral, President Clinton called it "fantastic." Because so many people came—5,000 of them—some had to be turned away.

About then, it seemed the first family was ready to open their gifts under the tree in the Yellow Oval Room, so I thanked them and left.

A New Year Dawns

Friday, January 7, 1994 – *A Sad Day*

My first day back after taking two consecutive sick days, the first time I've been off for two sick days in a row since working at the White House. I had a head cold, and could have pushed myself, but knowing not much was going on, and to spare the others, I thought it best to recuperate from home.

Early the previous morning, the president's mother Virginia Kelley had passed away in her sleep. What a lady. I had last seen her on Monday, December 27th, the day the entire family left for Arkansas. On that day, she was duly impressed with me because of a hot tip I received from a friend who happened to know that Mrs. Kelley had won $82 on the first race at Laurel Race Course in Maryland. Mrs. Kelly would often go to that track.

The prior Monday, the Kelley's got to the White House around 5 p.m. I greeted them at the South Portico and as we walked, I told Mrs. Kelley I'd heard she won $82 on the first race. She looked at me totally surprised and asked how I knew that. I told her, "I lived up in that area and I have my connections." Well, she got the biggest kick out of that and repeated the story to several others that evening.

I was sorry Mrs. Kelley was gone. I liked her most of the Clinton relatives—a real card. Roger Clinton is a good, down-to-earth fella. I remember how, at the Executive Residence staff Christmas party, he stayed late and entertained a lot of the shop personnel. Thoughtful!

***

At 8:55 p.m., I concluded a phone conversation with former First Lady Barbara Bush to cover some technical items related to her laptop. In that call, she invited me to come up to Maine for the upcoming summer. As the time got closer, she promised she'd send me a note with some dates.

Mrs. Bush sounded relaxed and rested.

January 11, 1994 – *A Voice from the Past*
At 8:30 p.m., I had an enjoyable conversation with former President Bush before speaking with Mrs. Bush. He answered the phone on the first ring.
George Bush (GB): "Hello."
Chris: "Hi, this is Chris Emery calling for Mrs. Bush."
GB: "Hi Chris, she's with our equivalent to Jean, our masseuse, right now. Can she call you back? I know she'd love to talk to you. Are you at home?"
Chris: "No, I'm at the office."
GB: "Well, can you call her back in fifteen minutes? She'll be done by then. Was there anything I could tell her?"
Chris: "No, I just wanted to talk to her about her computer. I heard she had a few problems."
GB: "Yes, she did, but I think it's all okay now. And I want to thank you for taking care of Marvin and Doro (his son and daughter). They reported back to me and said how nice it was to see you again."
I had set up a tour for them.
Chris: It was great seeing them, too. Walker (the grandson) is so big!
GB: "Yes, and how about Rob (Doro's son)?"
Chris: "He's tremendous! How have *you* been?"
GB: "Fine, great. Brent Scowcroft and I are leaving for China in the morning."
Chris: "Wow—for how long?"
GB: "We'll be there for ten days."
Chris: "That's great; so, you're doing okay?"
GB: "Oh ya—lots of travel, here and there. Well, please call back in fifteen minutes."

Friday, January 21, 1994 – *A Precious Meeting*
On this day, Katie, my eight-year-old daughter, came with me to the office. The Clintons were to go to Camp David, so I knew we could look forward to a relaxing weekend. Even though I was scheduled to work, it would be much less demanding with the first family away.

At 5:47 p.m., the president came to the State Floor to attend a staff event in the East Room. He stepped off the elevator, looked into my office, and saw Katie standing there. He motioned her over, stooping low to talk to her for a minute. He was very kind to her, and she was adorable, making it a very tender moment. The vice president walked with Mrs. Clinton near the entrance to the Cross Hall and watched as the president took his time talking with Katie. The president and Katie said goodbye to one another, then he joined Mrs. Clinton and the vice president. They proceeded to the East Room and shortly after left for Camp David.

Friday, January 28, 1994 – *Houseguests Coming and Going*

What a week! I worked days on Wednesday, Thursday, and Friday. Snow, sleet, and freezing rain have made this month challenging, with this week being a fine example. The previous two mornings, I got up at 4 a.m. to be sure I was the only *idiot* on the roads since they were so terrible.

***

The Clintons have so many houseguests coming and going, and more often than not, President and Mrs. Clinton are never informed by their staff that their guests are in the White House. Therefore, they often wouldn't see each other!

For example, the Clinton staff invited Mayors Rice from Seattle and Riley from Charleston while Mrs. Clinton was in Los Angeles. The two mayors arrived at 7 p.m., then went out to dinner and returned at 9:30. The president and Chelsea went downstairs to watch a movie at 8 p.m. These guests who stayed at the White House never got to say a word to a member of the first family! Clearly, the first lady's staff was still dropping the ball on simple but important things.

Tuesday, February 1, 1994 – *What's Going On?*

I was working evenings. Starting the previous day, the IN boxes used for President and Mrs. Clinton were relocated to the landing just outside of the elevator. As explained by Mrs. Clinton's aide, this was so the ushers don't walk into the West Sitting Hall and interfere with the first family's privacy.

The Presidential Protective Detail Secret Service agents were moved entirely out of the second-floor stairwell area for the first time in history; next, the ushers were told not to enter the Residence to deliver papers for the president. These were ill-informed decisions. In my opinion, President and Mrs. Clinton should have been examining their own staff and not be so concerned with the Secret Service and Residence staff.

In another interesting development, as the houseguests arrived last night, Mrs. Clinton's aide escorted them to their rooms instead of the usher on duty. More and more of an usher's traditional duties seemed to be in the process of being eliminated.

***

The previous night, the president came down a remarkable 10 minutes early to leave for a Democratic National Committee dinner. It took more than 10 minutes to muster up his staff to depart with him. While standing around waiting for them to get on the scene, President Clinton and I discussed college basketball. (It's great to have a basketball fan as president!) Once the staff finally showed, the president and his entourage left close to 10 minutes late!

Sunday, February 6, 1994 – *President Clinton is Angry—With Me!*
A crazy morning! I checked the usher log to see that President and Mrs. Clinton had been out late, returning in the wee hours of the morning. At the time, I had serious issues with the Executive Residence computer network, so I was busy figuring out the problem.

The president's running guests arrived at 8:20 a.m. so the lead Secret Service agent asked if I'd let the president know his guests were here. Knowing he was still asleep; I didn't want to wake him. But I continually checked with the butlers to see if they'd noticed any activity from him on the second floor. Nothing. Meanwhile, I was running back and forth from the Computer Room trying to get things fixed. I spoke to the running guests and explained that the president had arrived late and was sleeping in. Could they wait a bit longer?

They said they had no time constraints and added that the president had invited them for breakfast.

I thought. "Great! We didn't know anything about this!"

At 9 a.m. when I went up to the second floor, I could hear the shower running. I waited a few minutes until the water stopped, then I knocked on the door and told the president his running guests were here. Sounding perturbed, he asked, "What time did they arrive?"

"A little past eight o'clock."

He was suddenly angry and asked me why no one had called him. I said I didn't wake him because I knew he had gotten in late. I added that we'd given his guests coffee, hot chocolate, and juice.

"Who's down there?" he asked.

"Michael Driver, his son, and daughter."

I couldn't distinguish what he said next, but I could tell he was mad.

"I woke up several times, and just figured they weren't coming since no one called me," he continued.

"Sir, I apologize. I will go down and explain to them it was my fault and you didn't know they were here."

He said tersely, "Okay," and off I went to eat more crow.

***

When I got to the Diplomatic Reception Room, I couldn't find Mr. Driver. A Uniformed Secret Service Officer told me he'd gone running without the president.

"NO!"

Doing my best to maintain my cool, how do I now tell the president that his guest left without him?! I asked the Secret Service which way Mr. Driver went and was told he headed toward the East Wing. I took off in a run and, as I approached the far end of the East Wing near the exit to the White House, I saw a group of Secret Service Emergency Response Team members. Did they see anyone come that way? They all shook their heads no. "Great," I thought, "what do I do now?"

I turned and jogged back toward the Diplomatic Reception Room thinking, "Damn! There are six agents, one Uniform Division officer, a military aide, and other staff standing around here. How could they not know where Mr. Driver went?"

As I dashed by the Library, I happened to see Mr. Driver seated comfortably reading a book. What a relief! I explained the situation to him, then I went back upstairs to wait on the president. I propped open the double doors from the elevator to the main private residence hallway and waited there.

The president walked out wearing sweats carrying a cup of coffee. Still angry, he said shaking his head, "This late start messes up the whole day. How am I going to get to church now?"

"I'm sorry, Mr. President, I just didn't want to awaken you and Mrs. Clinton since you got in so late."

"We didn't get in late. It was midnight, and that's not late!"

As we rode down in the elevator, I asked about breakfast for the guests. Even more perturbed than before, the president looked at me and said again how everything was fouled up. "Well, I don't know what we can do now. Is anybody in the Kitchen?"

I thought, "Why is he asking? Of course, someone is there. Did he want things to get even worse?" But I responded said, "Yes, the chef is here. He can make breakfast."

"Well, okay." He was facing me in the ground floor hallway so no one could hear what he was saying. "We'll have breakfast in the Solarium in forty-five minutes, something simple. Chelsea and her friends won't eat much—bacon and eggs will be fine."

The president then walked up to the lead agent and said, "What happened this morning? I was awake at seven o'clock and then eight and then nine. Why didn't anyone tell me?" Before the agent could respond, I stepped up and said, "My fault, Mr. President. I apologize." He then walked over to Michael Driver and apologized to him. I watched as they walked out the South Portico doors. Wow, I really blew it!

Off they went, and I went back down to the Computer Room feeling nervous. The computer network issues were making matters worse.

***

I kept checking with the Secret Service on the ground floor so I wouldn't miss greeting the president when he returned. The Secret Service agents in the ground floor Staircase post told me I had at least 15 minutes, that he was shaking hands with people and hadn't turned back yet. So, I went back down to the Computer Room and, at 9:53 a.m., I called Staircase again. The agent said the president had just arrived and was upstairs. "Holy cow, I missed him!" I raced up to the Ushers Office and when I arrived, the agent there said the president had stopped by looking for me. Not good.

I quickly went up to the third floor to check on the guests, who were all there. But the president wasn't. I went back to the first floor and stood at the elevator. Finally, after five minutes, the elevator was called to the second floor. I jumped in and braced myself for more anger when the elevator doors opened.

Instead, Chelsea, two of her friends, and the president entered. He was laughing as he said, "Chris, you know it turned out to be a really good idea that you let me sleep in. My legs were so stiff out there running. I needed that extra sleep, so it's a good thing you didn't wake me up."

"Thank you, sir. That makes me feel better."

The president was still laughing as they exited the elevator and headed to the Solarium. I thought, "What a relief; I've got my job for a while longer."

Tuesday, February 8, 1994 – *Changes Afoot*
Chief Usher Gary Walters called Nancy Mitchell and me to his office and reported he'd had a meeting with Mrs. Clinton's Chief of Staff Maggie Williams. The decision to make a change in the White House Kitchen was announced. This involved firing all the chefs except for Pastry Chef Roland Mesnier and his assistant Franette. They even wanted to fire Adam, the long-time pot washer. Maggie Williams told Gary that the first family wasn't happy with the current staff and wanted to hire an American chef. The new chef would have the opportunity of hiring his own staff; the existing and soon-to-be former staff members could reapply for their jobs. She expected this change to be in place by mid-March. Given the rumors

circulating about the Residence staff, I asked Gary if the changes stopped there. He didn't know for sure, but he said another meeting would take place to discuss the operation of the Residence.

Gary and I then met with Chef Pierre Chambrin and informed him of his firing. I felt bad; Pierre was an excellent chef with a wonderful demeanor, and I hated to lose him. Pierre said he was not surprised, but what really bothered him was he replaced a chef who'd been in place 22 years. Pierre believed that he was doing a superior job but look what happened!

I agreed. Pierre had been the best chef since I'd come to the White House. He was so good to work with and always maintained control.

Before Gary's meeting with Maggie Williams, all types of rumors had circulated that Gary would be replaced in April. Were they getting Gary to do all the dirty work of firing personnel first, and then they'd fire Gary and perhaps his staff—ME? Later in the day as I was about to work out on the treadmill in the ushers' basement suite, housekeeper Chris Limerick told me to watch my back. I responded, "There's no back left to watch."

***

Thinking more about Gary's meeting with Maggie Williams, I doubt it was a two-way conversation. I got the impression she told him what would happen. Looking at the Executive Residence organization chart, I realized I could easily become the fall guy here. It's clearly depicted I'm in charge of the Events, specifically the chefs and butlers. This could well be the beginning of the end of my career at the White House. Philosophically, I thought, "It's been a fun eight years and a unique opportunity I took full advantage of." Little did I know what was coming.

Ironically, I remember sitting in the Ushers Office one year before telling the other ushers that the Clintons would be smart to wait a year and learn how we operate before making changes. Well ...

Monday, February 21, 1994 – *An Early Evening*
The president called and asked me to open the bowling alley, saying he and Hillary would be coming down to play. I turned on the lights and propped open the door. They arrived 15 minutes later. When the president saw John, the doorman, he said, "Why are you working on a Sunday?" Even though it was a Monday, but it was sad the president didn't realize we worked every day. He then said they'd be in for the evening, so we could both go home.

John and I decided to wait until after President and Mrs. Clinton finished bowling just in case they needed something. We still left early, about 8:35 p.m. My family couldn't believe it was only 9:30 when I got home. My then nine-year-old daughter, Katie, came running downstairs from her bedroom to hug me! What a great feeling to be home.

But it was short-lived. Twenty minutes later, the White House admin operator called and patched through a nervous staffer who had the president's schedule. I told her to leave it on the ushers' desk and the morning usher would take it up to the president.

"But the president gets up early!" she protested.

"The usher on duty gets in at five-forty-five in the morning, and that will be early enough. Good night."

Tuesday, February 22, 1994 – *A Satisfying Dinner*
A Clinton Administration first. A dinner for 21 people was scheduled in the Old Family Dining Room with senators, senior staff, and Mrs. Clinton. Even before the president came down, the social secretary and all her assistants had departed, followed minutes later by Mrs. Clinton's aides. Then once the guests were finally seated, my boss Gary left. With no "casts of thousands" staffers running around and rushing things, I was the only one left standing. What a great, relaxing dinner.

After the dinner, George Stephanopoulos came up to me and said how much he enjoyed the seafood. What kind of fish did we serve? Lobster and pheasant. He couldn't believe how good it tasted. Later, after the Clintons escorted their guests out and we rode up in the elevator together, President and Mrs. Clinton both remarked how much they enjoyed the dinner and dessert. Moments later, Mrs. Clinton called down to the Kitchen and reached Adam, the pot washer, who was the only person still working. She requested a second dessert. Adam called me and I called the butlers, who told me what I already knew—no desserts were left. Natalie, the pantry assistant, had packed all the leftovers and had given them to the staff. I told the butlers we needed to find something—quick! They searched through the Pastry Kitchen and found more of the Asparagus Surprise. Whew!

Wednesday, February 23, 1994 – *Meeting the President's Physician*

This evening featured dinner for 70—a normal routine with cocktails upstairs, guests roaming around, and dinner served in the Blue Room on the State Floor. The major difference was I wasn't stationed upstairs as usual; Curator Rex Scouten and assistant Angela did the honors.

After the dinner, the guests mixed and mingled in the Grand Foyer and hallway as the Marine Combo played. The president headed upstairs to use the bathroom. Well, I had a note from the duty physician with instructions for the president not to eat or drink anything after midnight, not even antacids. He was due to have tests in the morning.

I saw the elevator open and the president enter. I grabbed the doctor's note and dashed to the elevator to escort him. Just as I got there, Commerce Secretary Ron Brown jumped in and started talking to him about cellular phone deals. I could see all President Clinton wanted was a moment to relieve himself—and not have company. I gave the president his doctor's note as he and Ron Brown got off the elevator. He thanked me, and I made a quick exit to avoid hearing their discussion.

At 10:10 p.m., the houseguests arrived—Dr. Jack and Mrs. Karen Suen the president's personal physician from Little Rock and wife. He was Asian and she was 1000 percent Arkansan. I took them up to the Lincoln Bedroom and told them its history. We had a warm and engaging conversation. Dr. Suen asked my name, spelling and all, and said he wanted to write the president about my service to them during their visit. I thanked him, thinking, "YES! I can use the endorsement, buddy!"

Saturday, February 26, 1994 – *Is This What I Do Best?*
Chelsea hosted a party, 25 boys and 25 girls invited. But I had nothing to do with the setup of this party. I'm beginning to feel like an outsider. Do I earn $59,000 a year to only answer the telephones? Oh yeah, I still carry bags. As I was carrying the 38 sleeping bags and overnight bags to the elevator, I commented to the agents, "Yes, this is what I do best!"

Monday, February 28, 1994 – *History Lessons After Midnight*
While sitting in the White House's basement Computer Room, I took the time to compose some notes. The president was in Pittsburgh; Mrs. Clinton in New York. With Mrs. Clinton's aides traveling with her, things were quite peaceful. She was due back at 10:30 p.m.; the president was due back at 11:45 p.m. or later. British Prime Minister John Major was arriving with President Clinton and would overnight in the Lincoln Bedroom.

As the president and prime minister approached the Diplomatic Reception Room, the president looked at John and me then said, "I didn't expect to see you guys still here." As they entered, I welcomed Prime Minister Major to the White House, and he thanked me. I escorted the president, prime minister, and diplomat Roderick Lyne upstairs. As the president gave a tour, I waited. When the three men approached me about their accommodations, I said the prime minister would stay in the Lincoln Bedroom and Mr. Lyne in the Queen's Bedroom. President Clinton asked, "Now, wasn't the Queen's Bedroom Churchill's favorite?"

"Yes," I acknowledged. That piqued Prime Minister Major's interest.

As we entered the Queen's Bedroom, the president asked me to give a history, which I did, and then we crossed the hall to the Lincoln Bedroom where I told more history, which the prime minister found fascinating. Could I tell them about the Lincoln Sitting Room, too? The president asked. So, we all walked in there, and the president picked up a framed item.

"You know what this is?" he asked.

We looked at him for an answer.

"This is what was used to buy your way out of the draft during the Civil War." I couldn't believe the president of all people, given the persistent questions that came up during the campaign about his draft status, was drawing attention to this artifact! The guests were speechless as the president explained this script's history.

I then exited the room, and they were soon to follow. I stood out in the East Hall as President Clinton said, "Well, good night." I mentioned that breakfast would be at 8 a.m. The president then turned to John and me and said, "You guys have got to get home." I replied, "You bet!" With that, John and the president headed toward the West Sitting Hall. I asked Prime Minister Major and Mr. Lyne if they needed anything. They asked for water, which I told them was in a pitcher next to the bed in each of their rooms. The prime minister then asked if they could get tea at 7 a.m., and I said I'd take care of that. With that, I said, "Good night." Prime Minister Major smiled and replied, "Thanks a million."

Tuesday, March 1, 1994 – *Final Goodnight*

At about 11:30 p.m., the White House doctor called me to say the president had asked for Mylanta and she would bring it up to me. When I got it, I took it upstairs along with an envelope for the president that had come over from the West Wing. As I approached, I could hear the TV on in the sitting room. I walked to the doorway . . .

Chris: "Mr. President?"

POTUS: "Yeah."

Chris: "I've got your medicine from the doctor."

The University of Tennessee basketball game was on TV. Both President and Mrs. Clinton appeared from around the corner. He was dressed in a nylon jogging outfit; she was still dressed in the outfit she'd worn earlier that day. They both appeared to be fidgety. It was odd; they kept glancing at the TV instead of me.

POTUS: "Thanks. You can go on home; we're in for the night. Go ahead and turn off the lights."

Chris: "Goodnight."

That turned out to be my final interaction with the president and first lady.

Exiled

Thursday, March 3, 1994 *–Terminated*

My day began early; I was in the office at 5:15 a.m. I did some fine-tuning on the Executive Residence computer network and then got to the normal duties of the day. Thursdays featured pancakes for breakfast—always a treat for the staff to look forward to.

I finished eating by 7 a.m. and then took a walk through the State Floor. The Operations crew was rolling up the red carpet in the main hall and placing the stanchions in preparation for the daily public tours. Ricky McKinney, one of the ops guys, was singing Elvis: *"Well, that's alright, mama, that's all right for you; That's all right mama, just any way you do . . ."* Ricky sang Elvis songs just about every morning; he wasn't bad at it either, although sometimes he got a bit loud.

Under the Kennedy portrait, I saw Rockwood Peyton, one of the housemen. Rock, as everyone called him, was vacuuming, while Stewart Stevens was on a ladder in the Grand Foyer cleaning the chandelier. Several of the florists were busy placing new flower arrangements in all the State Floor rooms. Electrician Bill Cliber was adjusting the brightness of the lighting, while Chief Engineer Ed Windsor walked through checking the room temperatures with his handheld thermometer.

Meanwhile in the Pantry, Natalie Wallace was washing breakfast dishes while giving unsolicited advice to Maître D' Wilson Jerman, who was trying to get his coffee and make an escape! Executive Groundskeeper Irv Williams stood by listening and laughing. Such were the activities of a typical morning in the White House Executive Residence.

At 10 a.m., I attended an AIDS Awareness meeting in the Executive Office Building. On my way back to the Ushers Office, I stopped by Executive Residence Budget Administrator Worthington White's office to check on the status of my technology procurements.

Just past noon, I returned to the Ushers Office, and Chief Usher Gary Walters called me upstairs to his office. I ran up the steps and, as I walked in, and could see immediately he was upset. Gary looked directly at me and it seemed to take him forever to speak. Finally, he told me that Mrs. Clinton had told him she felt uncomfortable with me; that I was to be terminated effective tomorrow.

I stared blankly at Gary. What had I just heard?

He looked dazed. Then I began to grasp the severity of the situation and was becoming numb. My mind raced as I tried to think of something, anything, I might have done to warrant being fired from a job I loved so much. I swallowed hard and slowly began to focus.

Yes, I believed I had a good relationship with the Clintons, with never an indication of a problem. I pressed Gary for details. All he knew was what Mrs. Clinton had told him, the fact that she "felt uncomfortable" with me. Gary shook his head and added, "This is the hardest day of my career." I quipped that it was pretty bad for mine, too!

***

I thought about the staff and felt concerned for how they'd react. Yes, I was management, but I never had the typical supervisor-to-subordinate relationship. People on the Executive Residence staff had become my friends, my family. Historically, because there was low turnover in the Executive Residence, I found myself in an extremely rare situation. I'd always believed I'd be at the White House until I retired after 30 or more years.

Gary and I talked until there was nothing left to say. Because it didn't make sense for me to come back in the next day, I handed him my White House Pass. We shook hands and I said goodbye. When I went down to my office to get my coat, Nancy was at her desk. It was obvious she was aware of my situation. I could feel her stare as I grabbed my briefcase. When I turned and Nancy stood, she had tears in her eyes. She walked over and we hugged. Incredibly, I kept control of my emotions and told her everything would be okay. I kept telling myself to keep it together; I refused to create a spectacle.

After saying goodbye to Nancy, I walked down the back staircase and past my friend Uniformed Secret Service Officer Bill

Wallace at his post on the ground floor. All I wanted was to get out as quickly as possible without talking to anyone. I gave Bill a salute and quickly headed toward the East Wing. Bill called after me. I thought, "No!" But I stopped and slowly turned toward him. He walked up and asked me what I knew about all the rumors going around, something about some of the staff being fired. I said, "Rumors are rumors," and off I went.

***

As I walked along the East Colonnade, I looked out at the Jacqueline Kennedy Garden and beyond to the South Grounds. Everything looked so peaceful and magnificent. I thought I'd best savor this view for I may never be back.

I had a lump in my throat, but I kept convincing myself to hold my head high and walk out with dignity. I made it through the East Appointments gate, giving a quick nod to my Secret Service friends. As I got to my parking spot on East Executive Avenue, I noticed and then ignored Jim Selmon, one of the butlers, arriving for his evening shift. I couldn't bring myself to talk to him, so I refused to look up.

I drove off and called my wife from my car phone. I told her I had good news and bad news. The good news? "I'm off tomorrow."

***

That hour drive home seemed like it lasted forever. My mind wandered as I thought about everything that had happened. I kept going over the past several months, trying to recall clues, anything that would have caused Mrs. Clinton to fire me. Nothing came to mind; none of this made sense. Though it wasn't a total surprise, it was still a shock. Here I was, only the 18th usher since the 1880s and the first one ever to be fired.

When I arrived home, my family immediately comforted me. I began receiving phone calls of support from friends and former staffers. I even received a call from Mrs. Bush. How did she find out so quickly?

The Press Onslaught that Followed

Members of the media began calling me immediately after I'd been fired. Because I'd been accustomed to dealing with them in my role at the White House, at first, this didn't seem different. As always, I refused to discuss anything concerning the first family or the White House. They wanted to know why I was fired; I didn't have an answer.

Mrs. Clinton's office called to ask me to refer all calls to Maggie Williams, Mrs. Clinton's chief of staff. Wait! What!? Unbelievable! Hours earlier, Mrs. Clinton fired me and now I'm supposed to let her office handle my calls!?

The next few days were difficult as I tried to make sense out of these events. I couldn't stand not knowing exactly why Mrs. Clinton fired me, so I wrote the following letter:

President and Mrs. Clinton   March 8, 1994
The White House
1600 Pennsylvania Avenue
Washington, DC 20500

Dear President and Mrs. Clinton,

Since last Thursday, I have been agonizing over my termination from the White House.

If there was something serious enough to warrant my being fired, I need to know what it was so I never do it again. It is my hope that you will tell me in what way I made you uncomfortable.

I feel I served the White House well, I am confident that if you checked with your family, friends, and staff that had interactions with me, they would affirm my high degree of professionalism and competence.

I will look forward to your reply.
Thank you,

    Sincerely,

    Chris Emery

cc: Ms. Margaret Williams
       Mr. Mac McClarty

I mailed four separate copies of the letter with the cc's to Mrs. Clinton's and President Clinton's respective chiefs of staff. To this day, I have never received a response or acknowledgment.

* * *

I needed to avoid the media as much as possible, but I finally agreed to go on record when the *Washington Post* called me on March 11, 1994. The reporters asked for my reaction to an article being published in the next day's edition. Through their investigation, the *Post* had revealed I was fired because I had phone conversations with Barbara Bush. The *Post* reporters told me Mrs. Clinton's spokesman said I had exhibited an incredible lack of discretion in returning phone calls to the former first lady. They said the Clintons suggested I was passing on personal family secrets to Mrs. Bush.

The facts were these: Yes, I had returned two phone calls to Mrs. Bush. The calls were in reference to questions involving her personal computer, which I had configured for her in December 1992—nothing more than that! For Mrs. Clinton to suggest I was telling Barbara Bush personal stories about the Clintons is extreme paranoia. First, I would never ever do such a thing, and second, anyone who knows Barbara Bush knows she would never tolerate or listen to such nonsense!

In fact, I'm curious to know how the Clintons even knew I had talked to Mrs. Bush. Coincidently, I had also recently spoken with Nancy Reagan, Rosalynn Carter, Lady-Bird Johnson, and the Johnson daughters from the very same phone in the Ushers Office. It's been customary for White House ushers to have interactions with former first family members over various matters.

***

Once the *Washington Post* article hit the streets, the floodgates really opened. News magazines printed their own investigative reports similar to the *Post*'s. For the next several weeks, I received over 150 calls ranging from the *New York Times* to the major television networks. I also received calls from tabloid TV shows. A reporter from the *Times of London* appeared on my doorstep offering compensation for my story. I turned her down flat. Later, a news magazine camera crew showed up in my driveway. I refused to speak to any of them and turned down all offers, declaring I'd never sell my story to anyone. I even received calls and visits from literary agents and publishing companies. Once they realized I wouldn't write a revealing kiss-and-tell book, they dropped any interest.

I had agreed to interview for feature articles in the *Washington Post* (March 23, 1994) and *Baltimore Sun* (March 25, 1994) to put this entire episode behind me and get on with my life. With all subsequent press calls I received, I referred them to those articles and told them that was all I had to say.

Overall, I worked very, very hard to dissuade the press from making my firing a bigger story. Ethically, I would never capitalize on what I knew or what I saw, and I'd never do anything to tarnish the office of the president or the White House itself.

***

Over time, the number of calls died down. But several months later, the press again called about Clinton aide Carolyn Huber, who made a revelation out of finding the mysteriously lost Rose Law Firm billing records on the third floor of the White House private residence. The appearance of these records—the specific subject of several investigative subpoenas—ignited intense interest about how they surfaced and where they had been. Mrs. Clinton ended up making history by being the only first lady ever to testify before a Grand Jury. That occurred on January 27, 1996.

Because of this, I was invited to appear on ABC-TV's *Nightline*. The producers wanted someone who knew about the White House third floor where the records were found. Would I describe who would have had access to such an area? I would do it as long as no personal questions would be asked about President or Mrs. Clinton. The producers agreed. I appeared on the show, although I was disappointed Ted Koppel wasn't the host; it was Chris Bury. However, if you blinked, you would have missed my 20 seconds of describing the third floor "book room" where the lost billing records were discovered.

Because of the Rose Law Firm records discovery, I was also interviewed by Judge Ken Starr's Independent Counsel as well as New York Senator Alfonse D'Amato's staff. All of the congressional interviews were similar to the ABC *Nightline* interview. The questions focused on the physical characteristics of the "book room" and who typically had access to such an area.

***

Never having been out of work before, being unemployed was much more difficult than anything I'd ever experienced. With a wife and four children to support, the pressures on me were immense. My savings and checking accounts were nearing zero. I couldn't sleep, and I lost weight. At five-foot-eleven in height, I dropped to 143 pounds and looked ill. I suffered from migraine headaches and chronic back pain.

During that time, I did as much freelance computer consulting as I could and also went back to the University of Maryland to complete my bachelor's of science degree in Information Systems Management.

***

A full year passed from the time I had been fired until I finally landed a job with the Howard County, Maryland, government. Everything was returning to normal—almost. Two years and five months after being fired from the White House, I was again thrust into the spotlight with the press calling. This time, it had to do with the FBI Filegate fiasco. The House Government and Oversight Committee members were investigating the improper use of employee FBI background files by Clinton staff.

During my time in the Clinton White House, my background investigation had oddly been performed ahead of schedule. Members of the media told me FBI agent Dennis Sculimbrene stated in a Senate deposition that my FBI background check was ordered more than two and a half years early. Supposedly, it was an attempt by the Clinton White House to find something to use against me to fire me or harass me into resigning.

The facts were these: I received a top-secret clearance in early 1986; my five-year update was successfully completed in early 1991. In November 1993, I was asked to update and resubmit my security forms, which was two and a half years ahead of schedule. Along with the SF-86 (security form), I was given a list of 33 highly personal questions from Clinton White House Counsel Bernard Nussbaum. The questions included what church I attended and what clubs I belonged to. Although I had absolutely nothing to hide, in principle, I objected and did not respond. Never before had such questions been asked of a White House employee to my knowledge. I submitted my completed SF-86 and tax release forms on December 14, 1993, and I was fired on March 3, 1994. To this day, I have maintained a top-secret clearance and have never encountered any issues regarding my background investigations.

Because of the FBI Filegate scandal, the Independent Counsel, Senate Judiciary Committee, and other House committees interviewed me several times.

How frustrating that even though I already had an active top-secret clearance, I had to submit my security forms a full two and a half years ahead of normal. I was also subject to three random drug tests during my 14 months in the Clinton White House, which of course I passed. By comparison, during my seven years with the Reagan and Bush White Houses, I had been required to take a drug test only once.

Ironically, all this occurred while stories of widespread drug use among Clinton staff were ignored. In addition, scores of Clinton staff members had not received their security clearances, yet they were working inside the White House. It just didn't make sense.

Epilogue

September 2020

When I was hired to be a White House usher, my boss, Chief Usher Gary Walters, told me I'd be serving at the pleasure of the president. That the president could look at my tie and if he didn't like it, he could send me home to never come back. I'd have no recourse. Gary also told me there are only two ways ushers leave the White House—they retire, or they die. I remember joking that if I were to give notice, he would kill me—making that statement true!

Yes, I served at the pleasure of President; however, it was First Lady Hillary Clinton who terminated me. I don't believe President Clinton ever knew what happened. I had every intention of spending my entire career at the White House; the job was a natural fit for me. If I'd stayed, I'd be serving in my 34th year and thinking about retiring in the near future.

I've been told by those working in the Executive Residence these days that the format and structure of the Ushers Office changed after my firing. The Clintons gave more decisional oversight to the social secretary. Later, during the Obama Administration when more staff was added to the Ushers Office, contact with the first family by each usher was significantly diminished.

***

I retired in January 2020. I was very fortunate to enjoy many successes during my 42-year career (other than being out of work for one year following my firing). My experiences in the White House taught me valuable skills I continue to apply today, specifically in the areas of communications, diplomacy, tactfulness, working under pressure, and learning to never take oneself too seriously.

***

I hope you found these stories interesting. To let me know what you think, email me at: WhiteHouseUsher@gmail.com
Also visit: www.WhiteHouseUsher.com

Thank you,

Christopher B. Emery

Index

CPSIA information can be obtained
at www.ICGtesting.com
Printed in the USA
BVHW072241061021
618333BV00004B/236